FIVE MI
BEFORE YOU START

VOLUME 4

Daily Devotional Readings for Three Months

"THY WORD HAVE I HID IN MY HEART,

THAT I MIGHT NOT SIN AGAINST THEE."

Psalm 119:11.

PETER G. FLOYD

Series of devotional readings in
four volumes to cover a whole year.

MOORLEY'S BIBLE & Bookshop Ltd.

ISBN 0 86071 220 6

DEDICATED TO

THOSE BUSY PEOPLE WHO REALISE

THE TRUTH THAT:

"MAN DOES NOT LIVE BY BREAD ALONE,

BUT BY EVERY WORD THAT PROCEEDETH

OUT OF THE MOUTH OF THE LORD."

Deut. 8:3.

Acknowledgement has been made of the source of quotations given in these readings. In a few cases, however, our search has been in vain; we therefore crave the generous indulgence of those authors.

Each volume contains three sections with thirty days readings. You will find two readings at the end for use when a calendar month has 31 days.

P R E F A C E

We live in a world of rush. No sooner are we up, and we have to be out! Many and varied are the claims of life upon us all. Hours slip into days, days into weeks, and weeks into months and years. Have you ever reckoned up the number of minutes there are in one day?

$$24 \times 60 = 1{,}440!$$

We have called these books of daily devotional readings, FIVE MINUTES BEFORE YOU START, because they have been prepared for busy people. Not that anyone should limit their devotions to the time it takes for the seconds hand to traverse the face of a clock three hundred times! But surely, no matter how busy you are you can devote a short space of time each and every day to read the Scripture portion chosen, and the comment and hymn. Then as you pray remember that the value of prayer does not lie in the words we use so much as the sincerity of our hearts. A suggested prayer is given each day, read this over first and then pray the prayer from your heart. Other prayers, either liturgical or extempore, may follow.

It is absolutely essential for every Christian to set apart some time for daily personal devotions. Some may wish to spend longer in prayer, and if so you will find that what has been prepared here will make a good start for your daily QUIET TIME, and help toward a better understanding of the teachings to be found in the Word of God.

The aim has been for variety rather than continuity, although it will be observed that many of the days follow a certain theme. The comments are based on the text of the King James Authorised Version, but quite often helpful quotations from more modern translations are also given. You will find that sometimes extra thoughts and Scripture references have been given which could prove a help at any time you can spend in Bible study. The main purpose of these readings, however, is to help and encourage busy Christians in the good habit of a daily devotional life. As the apostle Peter says: *"Grow in grace and in the knowledge of our Lord and Saviour Jesus Christ."* I Peter 3:18. If you don't know you won't grow!

Having been a preacher of the Gospel of the grace of God for over fifty years, thirty seven of which were spent as the pastor of an Evangelical Church in South London, I have drawn upon personal experience and many illustrations given here are from my own personal life.

This quotation is from The Westminster Confession: "What is the chief end of man? Man's chief end is to glorify God, and to enjoy Him for ever." "Our souls are restless", said St. Augustine, "until they find their rest in Thee." How true that is! Unless your life is God-centred you will never know true heart-satisfaction. The most valuable minutes of each day are those you spend in the Presence of God. Get into the habit of spending time with God before you start the day.

The title given to these daily readings should, of course, be taken in a figurative sense. The suggestion is not intended to limit our devotions to five minutes but just a short while kept regularly for praise and prayer and Bible reading will be found to be most rewarding. Those who are new to the Christian Faith will soon discover that as a devotional time becomes established our desire for fellowship with the Lord increases. Determine to give God some of the time He gives to you.

Join the 2 Timothy 2:15 Club. Write for particulars to:-

The Fishers' Fellowship,
96 Plaistow Lane,
Bromley, Kent, BR1 3AS.

BETWEEN OURSELVES

As we come to the last volume in this series of Daily Devotional Readings, I wish to say how grateful I am for all the help and encouragement the Lord has graciously given me, first by seeing the fulfilment of a prophetic utterance He gave before I retired from the regular ministry of the church, and more recently through the many letters received from readers telling of the Lord's blessing in their personal lives through this ministry. To God be the glory!

During the past couple of decades many churches have re-named their weeknight meetings for prayer and fellowship by making use of the Greek word, KOINONIA. This word has been translated in the King James A.V. either by our Word, Communion, or Fellowship (compare for instance I Cor. 10:16-17 and II Cor. 13:14 where we read '*communion*' and I John 1:3, 5, 6 and 7 where we read, '*fellowship*'.) Koinonia really means, 'the joint-participation in something which is common to all', and is therefore a most descriptive word used to illustrate Christian Fellowship. (See also the warning in Eph. 5:11 and II Cor. 6:14). Fellowship and communion are two kinds of sharing which only believers can enjoy. One of the most amazing things about Christian Fellowship (Koinonia) is that distance is no hindrance. There can be a 'communion of saints' even when we are not together in bodily presence. I think it must be this truth which has caused many friends to write such expressions as: "Having read your little messages (some many times over) I feel I have got to know you." While other folk who have met me say: "As I read what you have written I can hear you saying it, and often the word comes 'alive'." Well, Thank God for Christian Koinonia, for this is just what is meant.

Sincerely yours in the fellowship of the Gospel.

Peter B. Lloyd

Hastings,
Sussex.

SECTION TEN

FIRST DAY

Read: Jeremiah 49:28-33

"DWELL DEEP" - v.30.

Personal testimony and up-to-date experiences - Days 1-10.

Did you understand much of this Scripture reading today? No! Neither did I at first, until I turned to my Bible Dictionary and a Commentary. But it didn't matter at the time whether I knew anything about the historical setting of these verses or not, it was simply those two little words that were such a help to me - *"DWELL DEEP"*. I do not recollect ever reading them before, although I must have done so, more than once! At the end of last year I had to go into hospital and have an operation; a dear friend of ours wrote such a kind letter to my wife and I, assuring us of her prayers; she also put in a slip from a scripture calendar. The date on it was Wednesday, 28th December (the day I went in) and the text was Jeremiah 49:30 with just these two words *"Dwell deep"*, and a comment by Mrs. Howard Taylor which ran: "Dwell deep - possess, as never before, the 'secret place of the Most High'. Occupied with the LORD - His beauty, His majesty and glory, His all-controlling and most blessed will. We shall find that He is indeed occupied with us - keeping, hiding, lifting up. Is not this just what we need?"

That little message came as the Lord's message for me just then. What blessings may come to us in times of need, simply through someone writing a letter and prayerfully passing on some such little word. "Dwell deep" - possess as never before the 'secret place of the Most High'. Occupied with the LORD." As I read those words over and over again, lying in that hospital bed, they became "meat and drink to my soul". I will tell you more tomorrow, but read that comment over slowly yourself now, and I am sure you will find something which will just meet your need for today.

Deeper, still deeper, into Thy love;
What else e'er charms me, Lord Jesus remove:
Earth clouds and self-will bid Thou depart;
Be Thou enthroned in this poor yearning heart.

Broken, more broken, fain would I be,
Ever remembering dark Calvary's tree,
Seeing Thy hands, Thy feet and Thy side,
Knowing naught else but my Lord crucified.

Higher, still higher, on faith's strong wings,
Till all my being exaltingly sings -
Praise, honour, glory, wisdom and might
Be unto Thee who turned darkness to light.

Rapture, yes rapture, when I shall rise
With glorious triumph through yonder skies;
Then shall I see Thee, belike Thee and reign
With Thee for ever, Thou blest Lamb once slain.

E. T. Mellor.

PRAYER

Almighty God, my living, loving Lord, I praise Thee for this reminder that all I need to do is to "dwell deep" in Thee. Keep me "in the secret place of the Most High" all through today, "abiding under the shadow of the Almighty." May Thy Name be honoured through my life, for Thy Name's sake. Amen.

SECOND DAY

Read: Psalm 91

"Shall abide under the shadow of the Almighty."
v.1.

Well, I still have it here in front of me - that slip from the calendar. Perhaps you would like to read it over again in yesterday's comment - "Dwell Deep". Don't you think it is wonderful to have friends who can write letters of sympathy and comfort when we are in need! Especially when we perceive that the heart behind the pen had been lifted to God in prayer. Often just the touch of a human hand, or the sharing of a human heart can go a long way towards recovery. That letter and its enclosure both played their part as far as I was concerned. Strange how two little words can grip the mind and feed the heart: "dwell deep", it said! As I lay in hospital there were times when I felt less well than I could have wished, but I found those words stilled the tempest, allayed my fears, and brought me back to calm. The physiotherapist had been to see me, and said "I am going to teach you how to breathe. Breathe deeply through your nose and out through your mouth. That's it, now again, and again. Now I want you to practise that, and when you come round after the anaesthetic do that a number of times, and it will help a lot." So that's it - breathe deeply and dwell deep. So it was that I found in my soul an undercurrent that seemed to carry me along both physically and spiritually. "Possess as never before the secret place of the Most High - occupied with the Lord, His beauty, His majesty, His glory, His all-controlling." That's what it means to dwell deep. Be occupied with the LORD, not my fears; His peace, not my frets about the surroundings; His faithfulness in every situation. In the war years many people in the district where I lived would go to Chislehurst caves every night. The homeland was bombarded but deep in the caves they were safe, and did not even hear the noise of battle! Lord, keep me dwelling deep; and I must breathe deeply too

There is a place of quiet rest,
Near to the heart of God:
A place where sin cannot molest,
Near to the heart of God.

O Jesus, blest Redeemer,
Sent from the heart of God,
Hold us who wait before Thee
Near to the heart of God.

There is a place of comfort sweet,
Near to the heart of God,
A place where we our Saviour meet,
Near to the heart of God.

There is a place of full release,
Near to the heart of God,
A place where all is joy and peace,
Near to the heart of God.

C. B. McAfee.

PRAYER

Blessed Lord, keep me in that place of restful trust that whatever may come, my life may reflect Thy glory. Amen.

THIRD DAY

Read: Romans 12:1-13

"Present your bodies a living sacrifice,
holy, acceptable unto God,
which is your reasonable service"
(or 'spiritual worship').

How good the Lord has been to me: had it been necessary for me to have this operation a year ago, I could not have gone through with it. It was then that I had that period of spiritual warfare and nervous exhaustion, related in the booklet "When Waves Swamp the Boat". There could be no comparison between my mental outlook as it was then and now. When I saw the consultant in November, and he suggested operating, I told him I would rather not have surgery if possible. Then he kindly explained to me his reasons, and I felt that he knew much more about my anatomy than I did, so I agreed on the strength of his advice. As I left the hospital these words came readily to mind: "Oh, rest in the LORD, wait patiently for Him, and He shall give thee thy heart's desire, and He shall give thee thy heart's desire." For some days I sang that over and over in my mind and felt it applied to my present experience. None of us can be said to enjoy the thought of an operation, but what calm assurance the Lord can give!

So the day came when I undressed and got into the hospital bed. A nurse soon came and took my temperature, pulse rate, and blood pressure, and the notes which were to record my progress were started. That afternoon a doctor came and examined me, then he gave me a form and pen with the request "Sign the consent form". I once heard an illustration about two kinds of faith, and have often used it. There is faith that takes, and faith that gives. You go to a doctor and he prescribes medicine, you have to have faith to take it whatever it is. I was now to exercise the other kind of faith - a faith that gives! In my case now medicine could not accomplish what was necessary. Now I had to give my body to the surgeon for him to do what he knew was best. When first we come to Christ we take Him to be our Saviour, that we call salvation. Then He asks us to present ourselves to Him for His service; this requires a faith that is willing to give oneself to the Lord - and that we call sanctification. God wants us to live in the constant experience of both. "Saved to serve".

Take my life and let it be
Consecrated, Lord, to Thee;
Take my moments, and my days,
Let them flow in ceaseless praise.

Take my will and make it Thine:
It shall be no longer mine;
Take my heart, it is Thine own:
It shall be Thy royal throne.

Take my love, my Lord I pour
At Thy feet its treasure store;
Take myself, and I will be
Ever, only, all for Thee.

Frances Ridley Havergal
(1836-1879).

PRAYER

Grant, O Lord, that I may not only show forth Thy praise with my lips, but by my life: that I may give myself to Thee, serving Thee in holiness and righteousness all my days, through Jesus Christ my Lord. Amen.

The Lord's Prayer.

FOURTH DAY

Read: Isaiah 40:28-31 & 41:10

"I WILL STRENGTHEN THEE"
41:10.

"No dinner for you today" said the charge nurse as I was being prepared to be 'put to sleep' for awhile; but I did not mind missing a meal. The quotation above came in a letter from another friend, miles away. *"I will strengthen thee"*. Yes, praise God, He does! Isaiah 41:10 has for years been one of my favourites. I like all those *"I WILLS"* of the Lord; what assurance they give! *"I will strengthen thee, I will help thee, yea, I will uphold thee with the right hand of my righteousness."* Another three hours went by and tea was being served: "Brown or white bread?" came the question. "No thank you, no tea for me today, I am due to go to the theatre." "Oh yes; sorry."

"Dwell deep". "Rest in the Lord". Breathe deeply. After another hour had passed a nurse came to give me the preliminary injection. It is now 4.30 and I am in the anti-room of the operating theatre; a lady doctor chatted about generalities: "What did I do before I retired? What part of London did I come from?" When I said south east, she said, "That's interesting, I lived at New Cross." Then you would know Zion Baptist Church." "Yes". "I have preached there".....I don't know what prompted her to choose that moment to put the needle in, whether she thought I might start preaching again, or what, all I know is that I did not know anything until I woke eight hours later with a nurse by the bed saying "It's all over, Mr. Floyd, you have come through fine." As it was past midnight I just went to sleep again until it was time for a cup of tea and a wash; then a boiled egg and bread and butter for breakfast. So it's all over; no complications, praise the Lord. That was what many of the Lord's people had been praying about, that there would be no complications. Nothing is quite so straightforward when one has "a concrete spine", as the surgeon called it when he looked at my X-ray plates. *"I will strengthen thee, I will help thee, yea, I will uphold thee with the right hand of my righteousness."* And He did, and does! So now before you pray, read that verse again, and place the emphasis on the words *"I"* - meaning God, and *"thee"* - meaning you! You will be sure to get a blessing from this verse my friend gave me in her letter.

Through all the changing scenes
of life,
In trouble and in joy,
The praises of my God shall still
My heart and tongue employ.

O magnify the Lord with me;
With me exalt His name.
When in distress to Him I called,
He to my rescue came.

O make but trial of His love,
Experience will decide
How blest are they, and only they
Who in His truth confide.

Tate & Brady.

PRAYER

O Lord, Thou art the God of deliverances to Thy people. We praise Thee for all the difficult circumstances of life through which Thou hast brought us. Thou hast delivered, and Thou wilt yet deliver; so we magnify Thy wonderful Name. Amen.

FIFTH DAY

Read: Hebrews 10:21-25 and Psalm 96

"O worship the Lord
in the beauty of holiness."
Psalm 96:9.

That was the text displayed on the wall behind the choir stalls and pulpit in the Baptist Church where I spent much of my youth. My favourite seat was in one of the side galleries near the pulpit, and from where I could see the organist, whose skills never ceased to fascinate me. What a blessing it is to be able to attend God's house and join in the fellowship of the redeemed! Regular attendance at the means of grace brings to us a steady build up of Bible knowledge, and helps to form Christian character. Little wonder then that the apostle exhorts us in the words of today's reading: *"Not forsaking the assembling of ourselves together, as the manner of some is."*

What a strange couple of Sundays were spent in hospital. I had rather been in the house of the Lord: it was radio and T.V. all day! Not too terribly loud, thank God, and how grateful I was that my bed was just inside the door and furtherest away from the T.V. set, so it was not so much a 'thorn in my spirit' as it might have been. To me this was a most unusual environment, but God can keep us in all circumstances. *"Dwell deep"!* Yes, deeper still: *"Occupied with the Lord, His beauty, His majesty, His glory."*

Thank God for the spiritual use of imagination: I was not able to meet with the Lord's people in person, but I did through this means 'look in' on many congregations known to me. Having read a Psalm I could pray for those who were just then gathered together in worship, and for those who were to minister the Word of the Lord - "O Lord, give Thy servants liberty in preaching through this day. May Thy word come to the hearers as *'Thus saith the LORD'*. Bring souls into Thy Kingdom, and may Thy children renew their strength as they wait upon Thee."

We praise God for our consecrated buildings, but God is by no means confined to our churches and chapels. He can be with you in hospital or Nursing Home; do not fret because you may not at present be able to meet in church as you have so often done: *"Worship the Lord in the beauty of holiness"; "Be occupied with the LORD, and you will know that He is occupied with you, keeping, hiding, lifting up."*

How pleased and blest was I
To hear the people cry:
Come! Let us seek our God today!
Yes, with a cheerful zeal
We haste to Zion's hill,
And there our vows and honours pay.

My tongue repeats her vows,
Peace to this sacred house,
For there my friends and kindred dwell!
And since my glorious God
Makes thee His blest abode,
My soul shall ever love Thee well.

Isaac Watts
(1674-1748).

PRAYER

The Lord's Prayer.

O Lord my God, prepare my heart to worship Thee in Spirit and in truth. Grant me true repentance and a living faith in my Redeemer. Write Thy word upon my heart, and fill me with the joy of Thy salvation, through Jesus Christ my Lord. Amen.

SIXTH DAY

Read: Psalm 41

"Thou wilt make all his bed in his sickness."
v.3.

LOOK UP! REACH UP! PULL UP!

This is about a special bed with a spiritual message! Often when I get into bed, I say "Thank God for a comfortable bed." I did not find the hospital bed very comfortable, but after a few days the charge nurse said "I think you would be more comfortable in that bed", indicating one further up the ward. So while I sat out, the one I had was exchanged for this bed especially adapted for the use of patients who had difficulty in moving themselves. I always thought it looked a good idea, when I had seen some patients in hospital beds which had a strap and handgrip hanging just above the head. Indeed it is a marvellous idea, and this bed also had a pedal at the side which a nurse could press down and the whole bed was slowly lowered so that it was much easier for me to swing my legs round and get out. Also, I am glad to say, it was a much more comfortable mattress. Now, with the help of that handgrip I could pull myself up into a more comfortable position whenever I had slipped down too low. Praise the Lord for a more comfortable bed! That handgrip hanging down overhead proved a wonderful blessing. It also taught me some spiritual lessons, and that is why I put at the top of this page LOOK UP, REACH UP and PULL UP.

Whenever I got into an uncomfortable position that is just what I had to do: look up and locate the handle; reach up and grip it, then pull up onto the pillows again. Ah! That's better!

"Thou wilt make all his bed in his sickness." A minister friend of mine visiting me when I was ill last year, read this Psalm, and before he prayed he said

"Spurgeon's comment on that verse is: 'Here we have three pillows - infinite power, infinite love and infinite wisdom'." So I looked up and located this hand grip waiting to be used, then I reached up and grasped it, and so was able to pull myself up again. What a spiritual lesson that taught me! When you are feeling down look up to God and locate one of His promises, then by faith grasp it tightly, and with its help pull yourself up once again, and on to those three blessed pillows - His infinite power, His infinite love, and His infinite wisdom. That's better, now you feel more spiritually comfortable I know. Whatever your need today, well or ill, be sure you LOOK UP, REACH UP, and PULL yourself UP. You will have a different outlook on life if you do!

Nearer, still nearer, close to Thy heart
Draw me my Saviour, so precious Thou art;
Fold me, O fold me close to Thy breast,
Shelter me safe in that Haven of Rest.

Nearer, still nearer, while life shall last,
Till all its struggles and trials are past,
Then through eternity ever I'll be
Nearer my Saviour, still nearer to Thee.

Mrs. C. H. Morris.

PRAYER

Almighty God, through whose love I am made nearer to Thee, help me at all times to look up to Thee, and by faith to grasp Thy precious promises, that by these I may become a partaker of Thy divine nature. O Lord, I do praise and worship Thee for Thine infinite power and love and wisdom. Amen.

SEVENTH DAY

Read: Psalm 34

"They looked unto Him and were lightened"
v.5.

"were radiant"
Amplified Bible.

It is truly amazing to see the amount of work our nurses get through, and they always seem so calm and take everything in their stride. The aptitude for nursing is born in some folk. Of course there are those in the nursing profession who are naturally better suited than others. Patience, kindness and cheerfulness I would say are three main qualities which need to go with the knowledge and nursing skills (that can only come with experience) to make a really good nurse. If to these can be added the ability to smile easily, then you have got the ideal person. Some folk possess a natural ability to smile readily, so that as soon as they come in they bring that happy sort of feeling we get when the sun breaks through on a dull day. We had on our ward a nurse with a smile like that: as soon as she came on duty the sun seemed to shine again. I noticed also she was often willing to 'go the second mile' to make sure her patients were comfortable. Doing a difficult job with a smile will lessen the difficulty and help to make the rough places smooth. I have here a verse card about that, and its heading reads:

THE VALUE OF A SMILE

"It costs nothing, but creates much;
It enriches those who receive without impoverishing those who give;
It happens in a flash and the memory of it sometimes lasts for ever.
None are so rich that they can get along without it;
None are so poor but are made richer for its benefit.

It is rest to the weary, sunshine to the sad,
And nature's best antidote for trouble.
It cannot be bought, borrowed or stolen
For it is something that is no earthly good
until it is given away;
And when it is given away, it always comes
back;
And nobody needs a smile so much as those who
have none to give."

Was it this the Psalmist had in mind when he wrote our verse for today? - *"They looked unto HIM and were radiant."* A smile from you may speak volumes even when you cannot say much. Look to the Lord, and radiate His grace to those around you.

There is sunshine in my soul today,
More glorious and bright
Than glows in any earthly sky,
For Jesus is my light.

There is springtime in my soul today:
For when the Lord is near,
The dove of peace sings in my heart,
The flowers of grace appear.

There is gladness in my soul today,
And hope, and peace, and love,
For blessings which He gives me now;
For joys laid up above.

E. E. Hewitt.

PRAYER

Blessed Lord, in these quiet moments I look to Thee in faith. May the light of Thy love fill my heart just now, and may that love be radiated to others this day, unto Thy praise and glory. Amen.

EIGHTH DAY

Read: Isaiah 53:1-9

"He was wounded for our transgressions"
v.5.

Some years ago I had the idea of writing a 'Thank You' leaflet, with a Gospel message which could be passed on to folk at appropriate moments. Whilst in hospital I was able to pass on dozens of these little tracts. I kept a few in the locker and in my dressing gown pocket, and whenever I felt the opportunity to be right, one was passed on here and there. I have given away hundreds of these and never yet had a refusal. In this leaflet I thank folk for their help especially to the disabled, and go on to tell this story:

"It was during the first world war that a Christian worker went up to a wounded soldier in the street, and said 'Thank you for being wounded for me'. The soldier looked at him in amazement. No one had ever said anything like that to him before. Many folk had sent cigarettes out to the soldiers, or knitted woollen socks for them to wear. Welfare workers had organised outings for these men during their convalescence, but nobody had ever said 'Thank you for being wounded for me'. It seemed to make it all so personal, and indeed it was! As these two men chatted by the curbside the stranger, whom the soldier now felt to be a new-found friend, went on to say: 'I can tell you of someone who wounded for you.' Then very simply and earnestly he told the story of Jesus, who was *"wounded for our transgressions; He was bruised for our iniquities....."* about the Son of God who lived a sinless life, and then suffered on the cross of Calvary for our sins - *"The just for the unjust, that He might bring us to God".*"

How much Jesus must have suffered for us! They put a crown of thorns on His head; *"He was despised and rejected of men."* They spat on Him and scourged Him;

then the soldiers drove great nails through His hands and feet. This soldier had heard about the wounds of Jesus before, but that day the message of the Saviour's love reached his heart in a new way. Have you thanked the Lord Jesus for being wounded for you?

Wounded for me, wounded for me,
There on the cross He was wounded for me:
Gone my transgressions and now I am free,
All because Jesus was wounded for me.

Risen for me, risen for me,
Up from the grave He has risen for me;
Now evermore from death's sting I am free,
All because Jesus has risen for me.

Living for me, living for me,
There on the Throne He is living for me;
Saved to the uttermost now I shall be,
All because Jesus is living for me.

Coming for me, coming for me,
One day to earth He is coming for me;
Then with what joy His dear face I shall see;
Oh, how I praise Him - He's coming for me.

G. W. R.

PRAYER

Lord Jesus, my Saviour, I thank Thee that Thou hast been wounded for me. I praise Thee that Thou art now living in the glory for me, and that someday Thou wilt come for me and I shall see Thee face to face. Until that glad day shall dawn, keep me faithful in my witness. Make me a channel of Thy love. Amen.

NINTH DAY

Read: Luke 11:1-13

"How much more shall your heavenly Father give the Holy Spirit to them that ask Him."
v.13.

It is hard to imagine life without the telephone, and yet it is only just over the last hundred years or so that this manner of communication has been used. I know those of us who have a telephone sometimes consider it a mixed blessing, but the blessings surely outweigh the few times it may ring at an awkward moment. When I found there was a portable plug-in telephone in the ward, I was so glad and grateful. Although my dear wife visited me every day, it was nice to be able to phone my own number and speak to her at home. I did not feel so far away knowing it was possible, for a few coppers, to have a chat or to ask for some little something I found I needed. Just to know that access was available was a tremendous help.

That's like prayer! Isn't it wonderful to know that through God's grace we can speak to Him whenever we wish. That is what prayer really is - talking to God, or I should say, talking with God, for prayer is no mere monologue! I am not now thinking of those times in church when we join with others in prayer, whether it be liturgical or extempore prayer, that truly is blessed, but don't you think it is even more blessed to know you can communicate at any time and anywhere with your Heavenly Father, who knows all about you, and loves and cares for you?

Our Lord gave this parable not to illustrate any such reluctance on God's part, but to set forth the principle of persistence in prayer. The key verse is v.13 *"How much more....."* If that man would only give because of his friend's importunity, then *"how much more"* is our God willing to answer our earnest prayers for blessing! Cultivate this habit of talking with God at any time and in any place. He is more willing to hear our prayers than we are to pray! That is the lesson He wants us to learn from today's reading. You may recollect the story of the little girl in Sunday School who was learning a new chorus:

God is still on the throne,
And He will remember His own.
Though trials may press us,
And burdens distress us,
He never will leave us alone.
God is still on the throne,
And He will remember His own;
His promise is true,
He will not forget you;
God is still on the throne.

A blessed truth this! But the little girl thought the first line was 'God is still on the phone'! Well, perhaps she was not so far wrong after all!

Don't stop praying! the Lord is nigh.
Don't stop praying, He'll hear your cry;
God has promised, and He is true, -
Don't stop praying; He'll answer you.

Don't stop praying, but have more trust;
Don't stop praying, for pray we must!
Faith will banish a mount of care;
Don't stop praying! God answers prayer.

Edna R. Worrell.

PRAYER

The Lord's Prayer.

Now, using your own words - pray; just talk with God. Don't forget the listening part of prayer!

<u>TENTH DAY</u>

<u>Read: Acts 28:16-31</u>

"And some believed the things which were spoken, and some believed not."

v.24.

As the days went by I was able to sit up for longer at a time, also to take some exercise by walking up and down the ward with the help of two Zimmer quad-sticks. This brought me into contact with other patients. It's interesting to see the various ways people react when one brings the conversation round to the things of the Lord. I never think it wise to 'force religion down people' as is sometimes said. I prefer to 'feel my way' with a person, and it soon becomes evident whether or not the word will be received. As I chatted with each one I tried to sense which of my little Comfort booklets would be most appropriate. 'The Greatest Friend', 'Beauty of Springtime', and 'Beside Still Waters' were the three most often used to leave with patients. It was just a means of 'sowing the seed', but when one man told me he had read all through my booklet 'Beside Still Waters', I felt encouraged, and we were able to have a further chat about spiritual things.

Some years ago I asked a friend of mine, who was an evangelist, how he got on when he had just concluded another ten-day campaign. His reply was simply "Well, some believed the things which were spoken, and some believed not." When the apostle Paul preached at Rome, as we have seen in today's reading, v.24, his preaching produced the same results: *"some believed the things which were spoken, and some believed not."* This is always the great divide! Our reaction to what God's Word declares is of tremendous importance. Verse 23 is most enlightening, and you will notice the nature of Paul's preaching: *"to whom he <u>expounded</u> and <u>testified</u> the Kingdom of God, <u>persuading them concerning Jesus</u>,* *both out of the law of Moses, and out of the prophets, from morning till evening."*

Think carefully about the words underlined, and you will learn much I feel sure. Paul's preaching was expositional, personal - testimony, persuading, about JESUS, and he had no New Testament to help him!

O Word of God incarnate,
O wisdom from on high,
O truth, unchanged, unchanging,
O Light of our dark sky:
We praise Thee for the radiance
That from the hallowed page,
A lantern to our footsteps
Shines on from age to age.

It floateth like a banner
Before God's host unfurled;
It shineth like a beacon
Above the darkling world;
It is the chart and compass
That o'er life's surging sea,
Mid mists and rocks and quicksands
Still guides, O Christ, to Thee.

William Walsham How
(1823-1897).

PRAYER

O Lord, I praise Thee for the written Word; may it always lead me to Christ, the Living Word. Grant such faith that my soul shall be saved, and sanctified, and satisfied, for the sake of Christ my Saviour and Lord.
Amen.

ELEVENTH DAY

Read: Luke 24:13-27

"And beginning at Moses, and all the prophets, he (Jesus) *expounded unto them in all the scriptures the things concerning himself."*

So you see it was not only Paul who preached Jesus from the Old Testament, as we saw yesterday, but the risen Lord had also expounded those things written in the scriptures concerning himself! There is a most useful little booklet, published by the Scripture Gift Mission (Eccleston Street, London, W.) entitled 'The Sufferings of the Messiah Foretold'. In it many O.T. passages are printed in one column with verses from the N.T. opposite, showing their fulfilment.

What a marvellous experience it must have been for those two disciples on the road to Emmaus, when Jesus revealed to them the teaching of scripture concerning Himself, "*Beginning at Moses*", we read - that is the first five books in our Bible, which we call the Pentateuch. - It is called "The Book of Moses" in II Chron. 25:4; Neh. 13:1 and Mark 12:26. Then Jesus turned to the prophets and showed that many things they wrote had been fulfilled in His life and death. Of course there were many times in our Lord's teaching when He either quoted from, or made reference to, the Old Testament scriptures. He spoke of Abraham, Isaac and Jacob; of Noah, David and Solomon. I will give just one passage where Jesus taught men about God's love and salvation by referring to Moses. You will find it in John 3:14-18: *"As Moses lifted up the serpent in the wilderness* (see Numbers 21) *even so must the Son of Man be lifted up* (that is on the cross) *that whosoever believeth in him should not perish, but have everlasting life."* Here our Lord drew upon an O.T. incident to illustrate the way we may be saved. Those people who looked to the brazen serpent, which God had commanded Moses to lift up on a pole, were healed from the result of being poisoned by the snakes. If we will look to

Jesus in faith we too will be saved from the poison of sin. How true it is that the Old and New Testaments are two parts of one whole. *"Man shall not live by bread alone"* said Jesus, *"but by every word that proceedeth out of the mouth of God."*

There is life for a look at the crucified One,
There is life at this moment for thee;
Then look, sinner, look unto Him and be saved,
Unto Him who was nailed to the tree.

Look! Look! look and live!
There is life for a look at the
crucified One;
There is life at this moment for thee.

Oh, why was He there as the bearer of sin,
If on Jesus thy sins were not laid?
Oh, why from His side flowed the sin-
cleansing blood,
If His dying thy debt has not paid?

Then take with rejoicing from Jesus at once
The life everlasting He gives,
And know with assurance thou never canst die,
Since Jesus, thy righteousness, lives.

Miss A. M. Hull.

PRAYER

Almighty God, we praise Thee that Thy Holy Word is always pointing us to Thy Son, who lived and died for our salvation. I praise Thee for the simplicity of the Gospel, and I put my trust in Thee. Amen.

TWELFTH DAY

Read: Exodus 3:13-14 & John 8:46-59

"I AM THAT I AM."
"Thus shalt thou say to the children of Israel, I AM hath sent me unto you."
Exodus 3:14.
"Before Abraham was, I am."
John 8:58.

You will see there is a vital link between Ex. 3 and John 8. Moses, when called to deliver God's people from Egypt asked the Lord: *"Who shall I say hath sent me? What is His name?"* Then God revealed Himself to Moses as *"I AM THAT I AM"*. This may sound a strange phrase at first, but it is a very important one, and interesting to know the implications of this explanation as to who God is. This is actually a phrase which gives the meaning of the name JEHOVAH. It means the One who was, and is, and will be; the Eternal. The self-existent One. He who does not depend upon another for His existence.

In John ch. 8, the Lord Jesus makes use of this *"I AM"* explanation of God, and applies it to Himself in such a way as to reveal His divine nature. *"If ye believe not that I AM* (the *"he"* in A.V. may be omitted as it is not in the original), *ye shall die in your sins."* John 8:24; *"before Abraham was, I am."* v.58.

I was interested to read that we find this phrase *"I AM"* a number of times in the O.T. God says *"I am thy shield and exceeding great reward."* (Gen. 15:1). *"I am the Almighty God."* Gen. 17:1. *"I am the God of Bethel."* Gen. 31:13. *"I am the LORD which sanctifieth you."* Lev. 20:8. And a number of other times.

It is very significant that the Lord Jesus in His earthly life and ministry made use of this title for deity in such a way that had He not been the divine Son of God, it would have been blasphemy. Yet each time

Jesus used it He revealed more and more of the purposes of God through His life. We will, during the next few days, consider these SEVEN GREAT "*I AM's*" of JESUS.

"I AM THE BREAD OF LIFE."
"I AM THE LIGHT OF THE WORLD."
"I AM THE DOOR."
"I AM THE GOOD SHEPHERD."
"I AM THE RESURRECTION AND THE LIFE."
"I AM THE WAY, THE TRUTH, AND THE LIFE."
"I AM THE TRUE VINE."

The God of Abraham praise,
Who reigns enthroned above;
Ancient of everlasting days,
And God of love!
Jehovah! great I AM:
By earth and heaven confessed;
I bow and bless the sacred Name,
For ever blest.

He by Himself hath sworn;
I on His oath depend;
I shall, on eagle's wings upborne,
To heaven ascend.
I shall behold His face,
I shall His power adore,
And sing the wonders of His grace
For evermore.

Thomas Olivers,
(1725-1799).

PRAYER

Teach us, good Lord, to serve Thee as Thou deservest; to give and not to count the cost; to fight and not to heed the wounds; to toil and not to seek for rest; to labour and not to ask for any reward save that of knowing that we do Thy will; through Jesus Christ our Lord. Amen.

THIRTEENTH DAY

Read: John 6:32-51

Jesus said *"I AM THE BREAD OF LIFE: HE THAT COMETH TO ME SHALL NEVER HUNGER, and he that believeth on me shall never thirst."* v.35.

Bread is the staple food of many nations. It may be made of wheat or barley or some other cereal, and in different countries it is customary to make bread in different ways. Yet its main purpose everywhere is to sustain life. It is sometimes called the staff of life. In this country we enjoy a great variety of foods, many of which are palatable, and yet we could just live on bread and water. We enjoy our food and like something rather more tasty, yet it is true that bread and water are basic to our requirements to sustain life. In the Gospels both bread and water are used to illustrate the requirements for spiritual sustenance. Read John 4:13-14 and note: *"The water that I shall give him shall be in him a well of water springing up into everlasting life."* Also John 7:37 *"If any man thirst let him come unto me and drink." "Whosoever will let him take of the water of life freely."* Rev. 22:17.

In the Gospel of John the Lord Jesus gives some wonderful teaching about Himself by the use of the phrase *"I AM"*. In fact He gives us seven metaphors: for instance, Jesus said *"I am the bread of life"*; *"I am the light of the world"*, etc. Today we shall consider our Lord as the Bread of life. In this verse 35 we have *"I am the bread of life; he that cometh* (notice the tense here - *'cometh'* - that is comes, and keeps on coming) *he that cometh to me shall never hunger; and he that believeth* (again believes and keeps on believing) *shall never thirst."* There is, of course, a sense in which it is true we are to hunger and thirst after God, and righteousness. This *"never hunger"*, *"never thirst"*, means such persons never *'go hungry'*; they will never be famished. It is good to have an appetite, and it's good to know how to satisfy it. As we feed upon God's Word, and all the wondrous perfections of the Lord Jesus, He becomes spiritual bread and our souls are nourished so that we become strong in the Faith. We need daily food for our bodies, we also need daily food for our souls, so that we never hunger and never thirst; we become satisfied in a spiritual sense. Never forget Jesus is the Bread of Life.

Break Thou the bread of life
  Dear Lord to me,
As Thou didst break the loaves
  Beside the sea;
Beyond the sacred page
  I seek Thee, Lord;
My spirit pants for Thee,
  O Living Word.

Thou art the Bread of Life
  O Lord, to me:
Thy Holy Word the truth
  That saveth me.
Give me to eat and live
  With Thee above;
Teach me to love Thy truth,
  For Thou art love.

Mary A. Lathbury,
(1841-1913).

PRAYER

The Lord's Prayer.

O Lord, I thank Thee that I can come, and keep on coming to Thee for spiritual food. Sustain and strengthen me. Quicken my faith to lay hold on Thee. Teach me how to "draw water out of the wells of salvation." This I ask for Jesus' sake. Amen.

FOURTEENTH DAY

Read: John 8:12-24

"I AM THE LIGHT OF THE WORLD; he that followeth me shall not walk in darkness, but shall have the light of life."
v.12.

You have only to read the first two verses in the Bible when you will come to these words: *"And God said, Let there be light: and there was light."* (v.3). When the Spirit of God moved and brought order out of chaos, the first thing was that by His Word God commanded the light to shine. Paul writing to the Corinthians (II Cor. 4:6) says: *"For God, who commanded the light to shine out of darkness, hath shined in our hearts to give the light of the knowledge of the glory of God in the face of Jesus Christ."* There cannot be sight without light, and we often use this term in connection with knowing and understanding something. We may say for instance: "Do you see what I mean?" In which case we do not refer to physical sight but to the person's understanding. This surely is the way in which Paul uses this word here: *"The light of the knowledge of the glory of God in the face of Jesus Christ"*, who is the LIGHT OF THE WORLD. God, who brought about natural light, now brings to us spiritual light. One of the greatest contrasts is that of LIGHT and DARKNESS; by their very nature they cannot co-exist. Light will expel the darkness from a room. The Lord Jesus said *"I am the Light of the world; he that followeth me shall not walk in darkness, but shall have the light of life."* Light and life go together; the light of the knowledge of the glory of God, revealed to men by the power of the Holy Spirit brings us into spiritual life. Note it is the one who follows Christ, *"the light of the world"*, who comes into the light of life. For this reason our Lord said *"Walk while ye have the light"*.....*"while ye have the light, believe in the light, that ye may be children of the light."* (see John 12:35-36).

"This is the condemnation, that light is come into the world, and men loved darkness rather than light, because their deeds were evil." John 3:19.

The whole world was lost in the darkness of sin,
The Light of the world is Jesus:
Like sunshine at noonday His glory shone in,
The Light of the world is Jesus.

Come to the light, 'tis shining for thee;
Sweetly the light has dawned upon me:
Once I was blind, but now I can see
The Light of the world is Jesus.

No darkness have we who in Jesus abide,
The Light of the world is Jesus;
We walk in the light when we follow our Guide,
The light of the world is Jesus.

Ye dwellers in darkness with sin-blinded eyes,
The Light of the world is Jesus;
Go, wash at His bidding, and light shall arise;
The Light of the world is Jesus.

P. P. Bliss.

PRAYER

Blessed Lord Jesus, I come to Thee; give me grace to walk in the light of Thy Word, that I may ever know the blessing of Thy fellowship. Lead others into Thy wonderful light. Amen.

The Lord's Prayer
(slowly and thoughtfully).

FIFTEENTH DAY

Read: John 10:1-10

"I AM THE DOOR: by me if any man enter in,
he shall be saved,
and shall go in and out and find pasture."
v.9.

Whether it be a tent or a palace, a cottage or cathedral, all need to have a door in order to function properly. Have you realised that the first part of any building we may approach to enter is the door! I know a good foundation is necessary, and a sound weatherproof roof, and adequate windows - all relatively important - but who would build a structure without a door? If entrance is to be gained to any building one must, normally, make use of the door; so this is of primary importance. Little wonder then that Jesus should make use of this metaphor, and say: *"I AM THE DOOR."* This comes, of course, in His parable about the shepherd and the sheep, and is an allusion to an eastern custom when a shepherd, having guided his flock into the fold at night, would often simply lie across the opening himself to keep them in and to guard their safety, thus becoming himself the door.

The Lord Jesus said *"I am come that they might have life, and that they might have it more abundantly."* v.10. You may recall that when God gave Moses instructions about the building of the tabernacle in the wilderness, it was so constructed that there was first the outer court made of fine twined linen erected upon poles all the way around, then the tabernacle, or tent, which had two compartments - the holy place and the most holy place where the glory of God rested upon the ark of the covenant. The outer court was about 100ft. in length, and 50ft. wide, with only one door called, in the A.V., a gate. This was simply more hanging curtains of fine twined linen; but it was to have needlework on it in three colours: blue, purple and scarlet. It was the only way in; anyone in their approach to God must enter that door with their sacrifice to be offered by the priest upon the altar of brass. That door of the Tabernacle can speak to us of Jesus, by whom alone we have access to God. Even the colours speak of Him: the blue - His heavenly, or divine nature; the scarlet - His earthly, or human nature; purple - the royal colour, a blending of the two. Instead of a hymn I will give you a little chorus I learned many years ago:

No other door; no other way;
No other Guide to the realms of day;
No other keeper when tempted to stray,
No other friend like J E S U S.

Y.L.C. Chorus.

PRAYER

Almighty God, my heavenly Father, I thank Thee for the Lord Jesus Christ through Whom I may come into Thy holy presence. Reveal Him as the Door to many, both young and old. Bless all who have gone into other lands with this great message of salvation. Bless those who are working and witnessing for Thee here. Keep me in Thy love and protect me this day, for Jesus Christ's sake. Amen.

SIXTEENTH DAY

Read: John 10:11-18 & 27-30

"I AM THE GOOD SHEPHERD: the good shepherd giveth his life for the sheep." v.11.

This is surely the most well known of all the *"I AM's"* of Jesus. *"I am the good shepherd."* It is in Isaiah 53:6 that men have been likened to sheep: *"All we like sheep have gone astray; we have turned every one to his own way."* Then we read about the shepherd: *"And the LORD* (JEHOVAH) *hath laid on him* (JESUS) *the iniquity of us all."* Jesus said: *"I lay down my life for the sheep."* John 10:15. As you read through this chapter you will see that Jesus contrasts the good shepherd, who cares for his sheep, and the *"hireling"* - a man who was merely employed to look after them. (See v.12-13.) A hireling would not risk his life if wild beasts attacked the flock; he would be more likely to run for his life. But the good shepherd would be faithful and true, willing to defend the sheep even at the risk of his own life.

When Jesus went on to say *"Other sheep I have which are not of this* (Jewish) *fold, them also I must bring,"* the Jews understanding He must mean sheep from the Gentiles, were offended and said Jesus had a devil, or was mad. (v.19-20.) Notice the Good Shepherd (the Lord Jesus) voluntarily laid down His life for the sheep. (v.15,17,18.) He said: *"No man taketh it from me."* When the Good Shepherd was on the cross, the people mocked Him, and the chief priests and scribes called out *"Let Christ the King of Israel descend now from the cross that we may see and believe."* (Mark 15:32). But Jesus was there, giving His life for the sheep and He could not come down because He would not! The Good Shepherd giveth His life for the sheep; He gave His all for us! *"He gave His life a ransom for many."* Mark 10:45. Note these four things about the Good Shepherd in John 10:

1. *"He gives His life for the sheep"*. v.15.

2. *"He knows His sheep"*. v.14,27.
3. *"He gives eternal life to them and they shall never perish"*. v.28.
4. *"He goes before them - always leading into green pastures"*. v.4,9.

Saviour, like a shepherd lead us:
Much we need Thy tender care;
In the pleasant pastures feed us,
For our use Thy fold prepare.
  Blessed Jesus, Blessed Jesus,
Thou hast bought us, Thine we are.

We are Thine, do Thou befriend us,
Be the Guardian of our way;
Keep Thy flock, from sin defend us,
Seek us when we go astray.
  Blessed Jesus, Blessed Jesus,
Hear Thy children when they pray.

Thou hast promised to receive us,
Poor and sinful though we be;
Thou hast mercy to relieve us,
Grace to cleanse, and power to free.
  Blessed Jesus, Blessed Jesus,
Let us early turn to Thee.

D. Thrup.

PRAYER

The Lord's Prayer.

May the God of peace that brought again from the dead our Lord Jesus, that great shepherd of the sheep, through the blood of the everlasting covenant, make me perfect in every good work to do Thy will. Amen.

SEVENTEENTH DAY

Read: John 11:1-7 & 20-27.

"I AM THE RESURRECTION AND THE LIFE."
v.25.

This whole chapter is one of those passages full of pathos, yet full of promise. We cannot stay long over the fact that Mary and Martha in their trouble sent for Jesus, and yet He did not come. It must have seemed such a mystery to their minds. There can be no doubt that these sisters thought, if only they could get a message to Jesus He would come at once. They had seen so much of His miraculous power that they quite thought the Lord would do something for them in their distress. Basically their trouble was much the same as is ours so often, they could not see the distant scene. They thought if only Jesus were present their brother would not die. In fact Martha said as much when she saw Jesus: *"Lord, if thou hadst been here, my brother had not died."* (v.21). The Master's reply was a veiled promise, *"Thy brother shall rise again."* To this Martha responded, *"I know he shall rise again in the resurrection at the last day."* But that, to her, was a long way off! Now will you please read the words of Jesus' reply very carefully, and with the emphasis on the two first words: *"Jesus said unto her, I AM the resurrection and the life."* Do you see what Jesus was telling her? She said, *"My brother shall rise....."* sometime in the future. While Jesus said, using the present tense, *"I AM THE RESURRECTION"*. He was saying, in effect, that for Lazarus the resurrection was going to be NOW! Jesus had all along had a plan, He now knew that in the sovereign purpose of God Lazarus would rise again from the dead, and it would be now. The power of the resurrection life of Jesus Christ was there and then to be shown. See verses 43 & 44.

On that first Easter Day the crucified Saviour became the Risen Lord. *"He that liveth and believeth in me shall never die."* That is in the spiritual sense.

Of course we must all die physically some day, but not spiritually, praise God! God gives to every believer eternal life. One day we shall know the complete redemption of our mortal bodies. Paul makes much of the hope of the resurrection in I Cor. 15. Because Jesus lives we shall live also, and we may know here and now the power of His resurrection life which will enable us to really live as "*new creatures in Christ Jesus*".

Low in the grave He lay;
Jesus my Saviour!
Waiting the coming day;
Jesus, my Lord!

Up from the grave He arose,
With a mighty triumph o'er
His foes;
He arose a Victor from the
dark domain,
And He lives for ever with
His saints to reign!
He arose, He arose,
Hallelujah! Christ arose!

Death could not keep his prey;
Jesus, my Saviour!
He tore the bars away;
Jesus, my Lord!

Robert Lowrey,
(1826-1899).

PRAYER

Almighty God I praise Thee for the great and glorious hope of the resurrection. By Thy grace enable me to live daily in the wondrous power of our Lord's resurrection, to the glory of Thy Holy name. Amen.

EIGHTEENTH DAY

Read: John 14:1-14

"*I AM THE WAY, THE TRUTH, AND THE LIFE.*"
v.6.

The green pastureland of John 14 has been well trodden by saints in many generations! Here we have rest for the weary, comfort for the sad, and hope that shines more brightly the older we get! *"Let not your heart be troubled, ye believe in God believe also in me. In my Father's house are many mansions - abiding places." "I go to prepare a place for you.....and I will come again."* What blessed words! They have been a means of strength and comfort ever since our Lord first spoke them, at the close of the Last Supper. Jesus intimated that He was to leave those disciples. Thomas said, *"Where are you going, how can we know the way?"* It was in answer to that question that Jesus gave this grand assurance: *"I am the way, the truth, and the life, no man cometh unto the Father but by me."* I read this recently, and it is worth remembering:

"Without the Way, there is no going;
Without the Truth, there is no knowing;
Without the Life, there is no growing."

We have seen that Jesus is the Door by which we enter the sheepfold, He is also the Way by which we get there. All spiritual experience of any worth begins with Jesus! Apart from HIM there is no going, and we progress more as we get to know Him better. All divine revelation comes through the Lord Jesus Christ. *"God hath spoken unto us by His Son."* Hebrews 1:1. The way to God is through Him, who is the truth of God. Also all spiritual growth is the result of His life in the hearts of believers. The more we abide in Him and draw upon His life and power the greater will be our spiritual growth in grace. It is most blessed to really know Jesus in this three-fold manner - The WAY, The TRUTH and The LIFE. He is the way to God, He is the truth of God and He is the life of God. And it is He who has gone before to prepare for us an abiding place in heaven. Truly did Jesus say: *"He that hath seen me hath seen the Father."* Jesus was the true revelation of God who came among us, and who is to take us to Himself. Blessed hope, blessed joy, blessed rest!

Teach me Thy way, O Lord,
  Teach me Thy way!
Thy gracious aid afford,
  Teach me Thy way!
Help me to walk aright,
  More by faith, less by sight;
Lead me with heavenly light;
  Teach me Thy way.

When doubts and fears arise,
  Teach me Thy way!
When storms o'erspread the skies,
  Teach me Thy way!
Shine through the cloud and rain,
  Through sorrow, toil, and pain;
Make Thou my pathway plain,
  Teach me Thy way!

B. M. Ramsey.

PRAYER

The Lord's Prayer.

Almighty God, I praise Thy Name that the Lord Jesus is to me, The Way, The Truth and The Life. I thank Thee for the love that sought me, for the blood that bought me, and for the grace that brought me to the fold.

Amen.

NINETEENTH DAY

Read: John 15:1-8

"I AM THE TRUE VINE."
v.1.

In order that we might understand the full significance of this declaration of the Lord Jesus, we must turn to the Old Testament. In Jeremiah 2:21 God, through the prophet, is calling His people back from their idolatory and says: *"I had planted thee a noble vine, wholly a right seed: how then art thou turned into the degenerate plant of a strange vine unto me?"* Also in Hosea 10:1 *"Israel is an empty vine."* God had planted His chosen people in the land as a good vine, but they forsook Jehovah and turned to the gods of the nations around them. They had become a degenerate plant of a strange vine. Even when Christ came to His own people, they rejected Him (see John 1:11 & 12). So now, at the end of His ministry here on earth He tells His disciples that HE is the TRUE vine, as distinct from the *'degenerate vine'* - the nation Israel.

In proof of this fact we read of our Lord, He always did the Father's will; He spoke the Father's Words; He manifested the Father's works. His was a life of spiritual fruitfulness, and that fruit remains. Although He was crucified, He arose from the dead, and lives again working in and through His own followers whose relationship to Him is that of branches in the vine. There could be no greater illustration of spiritual unity - ONENESS - than a vine and its branches. If by God's grace you have received the Lord Jesus Christ into your heart as your own personal Saviour, then you are a branch in HIM. His life is within you and you bring forth, what Paul calls in Galatians 5:22-23 *"THE FRUIT OF THE SPIRIT."* Jesus said we must abide in Him in order that fruit may be found in our lives.

"Just as no branch can bear fruit of itself without abiding in (virtually united to) *the vine, neither can*

you bear fruit unless you abide in Me." (verse 4. Amp.) Those who bear no fruit are merely professing Christians. All who have received Christ are branches in Him, but there are degrees of fruitfulness; notice in this passage the following: *"no fruit"; "fruit"; "more fruit";* and *"much fruit"*.

Jesus, Thine all-victorious love
  Shed in my heart abroad;
Then shall my heart no longer rove,
  Rooted and fixed in God.

Oh, that in me the sacred fire
  Might now begin to glow;
Burn up the dross of base desire,
  And make the mountains flow.

Thou, who at Pentecost didst fall,
  Do Thou my sins consume;
Come, Holy Ghost, for Thee I call;
  Spirit of burning, come.

Refining fire, go through my heart,
  Illuminate my soul;
Scatter Thy life through every part,
  And sanctify the whole.

Charles Wesley,
(1707-1788).

PRAYER

The Lord's Prayer.

Heavenly Father, by Thy grace and through the indwelling of Thy Spirit, enable me to so abide in Christ that the fruit of the Spirit shall abound in my life to Thy glory. Amen.

TWENTIETH DAY

Read: John 8:20-36

LIVING THE ABIDING LIFE.

"If the Son shall make you free, ye shall be free indeed." v.36.

Under this title we shall, for the next few days, consider what it means to abide in Christ. Jesus said, *"If ye continue in my word then are ye my disciples indeed; and ye shall know the truth, and the truth shall make you free."* (v.32).

Living the abiding life means, first of all, living daily in the freedom of God's Spirit. Never think of the teachings of Jesus as being shackles placed upon you. Being a Christian does not mean living bound under a series of prohibitions. Some have had the idea that to really live as Jesus would have us live must mean living a very restricted life. The fact is that the very opposite is true! Oh, of course there are things we do not indulge in when we become followers of the Lord, but it is quite wrong to place the emphasis upon the things we no longer do. There are, indeed, many things we no longer wish to do! Our Lord renovates our lives. He makes us a new creation, and the nearer we live to Jesus the more full and satisfying life becomes.

When I know that fire burns, and to burn myself gives me pain, I am not likely to deliberately put my hand on a hot stove. I may do so in a moment of carelessness, but I certainly would not choose to do so! It is like that with us and temptation. The new life within us gives us warning; the truth sets us free. Notice in verses 32 and 36 we have the word *'FREE'* three times over. Read both verses again now and note, Free! Free! Free! It is the TRUTH that makes us free. If the Son, Jesus Christ who is the truth, shall make you free, you shall be free indeed. And this spiritual freedom becomes greater the more we learn of Him. This is how it works: When I know the truth that God has forgiven me, I am free from an accusing conscience. When I know that as I keep my mind stayed upon the Lord I can enjoy His peace (see Isaiah 26:3). I am made free from fear and gloom. *"If ye continue in my word, then are ye my disciples indeed."* To continue is to abide, dwell, remain, rest in the Lord Jesus.

Abiding, oh, so wondrous sweet!
I'm resting at the Saviour's feet;
I trust in Him, I'm satisfied!
I'm resting in the Crucified!

He speaks, and by His word is given
His peace, a rich foretaste of heaven;
Not as the world, He peace doth give;
'Tis through this hope my soul shall live.

I live, but through His grace alone
By whom the mighty work is done;
Dead to myself, alive to Him,
I count all loss His rest to win.

Now rest, my heart, the work is done,
I'm saved by faith through Christ the Son!
Let every power my soul employ
To tell the world my peace and joy.

C. B. J. Root.

PRAYER

Blessed Lord Jesus, I praise Thy holy name that by Thy grace I have been brought into this glorious freedom. Make me careful to let Thy word abide in my heart that I shall truly know Thou dost set me free. Amen.

TWENTY-FIRST DAY

Read: John 15:8-17

LIVING THE ABIDING LIFE.

"If ye keep my commandments ye shall abide in my love; even as I have kept my Father's commandments, and abide in his love."

v.10.

What blessed union! What a glorious and marvellous privilege to abide in Jesus' love, as He abides in the Father's love! How can we possibly do that? By keeping His commands, and simply doing as He said we should. The secret of a happy, harmonious Christian life lies in abiding - that is remaining - in Christ. In the first ten verses we have this thought repeated eight times: v.4 *'abide'*, twice; v.5 *'abideth not'*; v.7 *'abide'*, twice; v.9 *'continue'*; v.10 *'abide*, twice. The reason for this emphasis on our abiding in Christ is because without HIM we can do nothing! v.5. Our usefulness as Christians depends upon our remaining in touch with the Lord. This illustration may help: Some time ago someone gave me a most useful little gift, it is a small sponge in a rubber container, very helpful when one has a lot of letters to be stamped as it saves an awful lot of licks! As I looked at that useful office aid, I saw a spiritual lesson for my soul. If that sponge is to be useful, and used for the purpose for which it was made, all it has to do is to remain wet. The sponge is in the water, and the water is in the sponge; if it gets dry it becomes useless. Its usefulness lies in its abiding in the water so that the water can remain in the sponge - that's all, I do the rest. Without me it cannot stick the stamps on my letters, but so long as it is wet I find it a tremendous help. If our lives are to be useful to the Lord, we must abide. Simply rest in Him like the sponge does in the water, we in Him and He in us, and moment by moment we are kept in His love. The greatest aid to our abiding in Christ is to daily read God's Word and lift our hearts to Him in prayer. As well as these quiet moments before you start the day, seek to practise what I like to call 'conversational prayer'. There is a lot of truth in that little chorus many of us learned in the Primary Sunday School, "A little talk with Jesus makes it right, all right."

Dying with Jesus, by death reckoned mine;
Living with Jesus a new life divine;
Looking to Jesus till glory doth shine;
Moment by moment, O Lord, I am Thine.

Moment by moment I'm kept in His love,
Moment by moment I've life from above;
Looking to Jesus till glory doth shine;
Moment by moment, O Lord, I am Thine.

Never a trial that He is not there;
Never a burden that He doth not bear;
Never a sorrow that He doth not share -
Moment by moment I'm under His care.

D. W. Whittle.

PRAYER

O God of peace, who hast taught us that in returning and rest we shall be saved, in quietness and confidence shall be our strength; by the might of Thy Spirit lift us, we pray Thee, to Thy presence, where we may be still and know that Thou art God; through Jesus Christ our Lord. Amen.

TWENTY-SECOND DAY

Read: John 15:11-27

LIVING THE ABIDING LIFE.

*"These things have I spoken unto you,
that my joy might remain in you,
and that your joy might be full."*
v.11.

Yes, there has been a little overlapping in today's reading, but verse 11 needs all the emphasis we can give it. You will note the Saviour speaks of two kinds of joy - His joy and ours. I like the Amplified Bible here: *"I have told you these things that my joy and delight may be in you, and that your joy and gladness may be full measure and complete and overflowing."*

My joy. Your joy. If the Saviour's joy and delight is in us because we are living the abiding life, then our joy and gladness will be complete and overflowing! What a thought! You can give JOY to Jesus! The more resolutely we follow His Word and abide in Him, the greater will be the fruitfulness in our lives, and the more God will be glorified through us. This is what the Lord Jesus is looking for, and this gives Him joy and delight. May I illustrate it like this: A loving husband does not buy his wife nice Birthday presents in order to give himself pleasure, his motive would, of course, be to give his wife joy, but when he sees how pleased she is that makes him happy too. By our obedience to the Lord Jesus, His joy remains in us and our joy becomes full - it overflows. As each day we read His Word seeking to know what He is teaching, as every morning we commit our lives afresh to Him in our prayers, we will be abiding in Him. Thus living in this right relationship with the Master our lives will be lived for His glory, not our own, and His peace and joy will dwell within us and flow through us to others for *"no man liveth unto himself"*.

There's a peace in my heart that the world never gave,
A peace it cannot take away;
Though trials of life may surround like a cloud,
I've a peace that has come here to stay!

> Constantly abiding, Jesus is mine;
> Constantly abiding, rapture divine,
> He never leaves me lonely,
> Whispers, Oh, so kind;
> 'I will never leave thee',
> Jesus is mine!

All the world seemed to sing of a Saviour and King,
When peace sweetly came to my heart;
Troubles fled away, and my night turned to day,
Blessed Jesus, how glorious Thou art!

This treasure I have in a temple of clay,
While here on His footstool I roam;
But He's coming to take me some glorious day,
Over there to my heavenly home!

Mrs. W. L. Murphy.

PRAYER

Blessed Lord, and Master, until that glad day shall dawn keep me constantly abiding in Thee. Teach me Thy way, O Lord, that I may bring joy to Thy heart and my life may be fruitful for Thy praise. Amen.

TWENTY-THIRD DAY

Read: 1 John 2:1-10

LIVING THE ABIDING LIFE.

"He that saith he abideth in him ought himself so to walk, even as he walked."

v.6.

"He that loveth his brother abideth in the light."

v.10.

The apostle John has been called the apostle of love. In his first letter John has quite a lot to say about abiding in the Lord. In verse 6 he points out that care must be taken in order that those who profess to be followers of Jesus will show it by the way they live. Of course, the absolutely perfect life Jesus lived here on earth was unique, but however much we may fall short of such utter and absolute perfection, we must keep watchful and seek by God's grace to live well pleasing to Him.

To abide in Christ is to abide in the light (v.10). See also 1 John 1:7 *"If we walk in the light as he is in the light, we have fellowship one with another, and the blood of Jesus Christ his Son cleanseth us from all sin."* Cleanses and goes on cleansing: *"Is all the time keeping us clean"*, as one writer puts it. Jesus is the LIGHT OF THE WORLD and we must follow the beam of light which He sheds on our path, never turning aside from it. As we do so our hearts will become loving toward others (see again v.10.) To abide in LIGHT is to abide in LOVE. A most helpful book on this subject of abiding is entitled, "The Three-fold Secret of the Holy Spirit", by James McConkey, in it he says: "Through faith the divine life flows to us; through love the divine life flows through us to others. To abide in Christ is to live a life of constant faith Christward, and of constant love manward."

"Let us love one another", says John, *"for love is of God"*. This is the way we can become channels through which the love of God can flow to those around us. Read verse 18 of chapter 3. J. B. Phillips: "My children let us love not merely in theory or in words - let us love in sincerity and in practice!"

Walk in the light, so shalt thou know
That fellowship of love
His Spirit only can bestow,
Who reigns in light above.

Walk in the light, and thou shalt find
Thy heart made truly His,
Who dwells in cloudless light enshrined,
In Whom no darkness is.

Walk in the light, and sin abhorred
Shall ne'er defile again;
The blood of Jesus Christ the Lord
Shall cleanse from every stain.

Walk in the light, thy path shall be
Peaceful, serene, and bright;
For God, by grace, shall dwell in thee,
And God Himself is Light.

Bernard Barton.

PRAYER

Almighty God, help me by Thy Holy Spirit to live this day, "Walking in the light" of this, Thy Word. Keep me living the abiding life. Fill my heart with Thy love. Give me a love for the lost, and for those whom I may feel are unlovely. Just make my heart a channel of Thy love, through Jesus Christ my Lord. Amen.

TWENTY-FOURTH DAY

Read: 1 John 2:11-20

LIVING THE ABIDING LIFE.

"Love not the world, neither the things that are in the world. If any man love the world the love of the Father is not in him."....."The world passeth away, ...but he THAT DOETH THE WILL OF GOD abideth for ever."
v.15 & 17.

Eternal life is the life of God. *"From everlasting to everlasting Thou art God."* Psalm 90:2. By virtue of our union with Christ we too shall abide for ever. Note, *"He that doeth the will of God abideth for ever."* And the person who does God's will is the one who *"abides in Christ"*. Abundant, full, and perfect salvation is ours through the victory of Christ. *"I am come that they might have life and that they might have it more abundantly."* (John 10:10.) The things of this world are only passing. There will be a time when the *"lust of the flesh, the lust of the eyes, and the pride of life"* - that trinity of evil - will pass away, but Christ is eternal, and those who abide in Him, doing His will, and partaking of His nature, shall abide for ever. So much depends upon the direction of the will. If we, with humble and contrite hearts sincerely desire to do the will of God, He will give us spiritual strength and enable us to do so. We read in Micah 6:8. *"He hath shewed thee, O man, what is good; and what doth the Lord require of thee, but to do justly, and to love mercy, and to walk humbly with thy God."* Here we find the trinity of good, *"To do justly, to love mercy, and to walk humbly with thy God."* This is the very opposite of the trinity of evil seen in 1 John 2:16. We might say, Micah 6:8 is the outward evidence of abiding in Christ. Such evidence of life comes from the fact that the life of Christ is flowing through the one who is abiding in Him. Paul set forth this truth in Gal. 2:20. *"I am crucified with Christ: nevertheless I live; yet not I, but CHRIST LIVETH IN ME: and the life I now live in the flesh I live by the faith of the Son of God, who loved me and gave himself for me."* What a blessed truth!

Living for Jesus a life that is true,
Striving to please Him in all that I do;
Yielding allegiance, glad hearted and free,
This is the pathway of blessing for me.

O Jesus, Lord, and Saviour,
I give myself to Thee;
For Thou, in Thine atonement,
Didst give Thyself for me;
I own no other Master,
My heart shall be Thy throne,
My life I give, henceforth to live,
O Christ, for Thee alone.

Living for Jesus who died in my place,
Bearing on Calvary my sin and disgrace,
Such love constrains me to answer His call,
Follow His leading and give Him my all.

Living for Jesus wherever I am,
Doing each duty in His Holy Name,
Willing to suffer affliction and loss,
Deeming each trial a part of my cross.

T. O. Chisholm.

PRAYER

Blessed Lord, my God, I ask Thee to make me know Thy will for me this day. Whatever task Thou hast for me, whatever plan, may I fulfil it unto Thy praise and glory. Amen.

The Lord's Prayer.

TWENTY-FIFTH DAY

Read: 1 John 2:21-29

LIVING THE ABIDING LIFE.

"Let that therefore remain in you which ye have heard from the beginning. If that....shall remain in you, ye shall continue in the Son and in the Father."

v.24.

To abide simply means to remain, to continue, and all we really have to do is to let that message of grace which we received at the beginning - when we first came into the experience of saving grace remain in our hearts. Let it remain. Water the seed by prayer, keep away the weeds of doubt by faith, and in the sunshine of God's love the word planted in the heart will flourish and grow.

Last year my wife put some pansy plants in the garden, and they were beautiful. This year also they blossomed profusely yet all we did was to let them remain in the soil. We did not dig them up several times to see if the roots were growing, or to make sure they were healthy. We just let them continue in the flower bed, and I have never seen so many pansies. You know, it is quite possible to become too concerned as to whether you are living the abiding life, wondering if you are still growing in grace so that you cease to enjoy the rest of faith which is yours through the sovereign grace of God. C. H. Spurgeon once said, "I looked to the Lord and the dove of peace flew into my breast; I looked at the dove, and it flew away!" Oh, how true that can be! We must never be over-concerned with ourselves, not even to see if we are in that spiritual condition we hope for. We must be more taken up with the LORD and all He is, then as we continue looking unto Him we shall grow more like Him. This is indeed an important point in living the abiding life. As the apostle Paul wrote to the Corinthians 3: 18. *"We all with unveiled face beholding, as in a glass, the glory of the Lord, are changed into the same image, from glory to glory, even as by the Spirit of the Lord."*

My heart is resting, O my God,
I will give thanks and sing;
My heart is at the secret source
Of every precious thing.

Now the frail vessel Thou hast made,
No hand but Thine can fill;
The waters of the earth have failed,
And I am thirsty still.

I thirst for springs of heavenly life,
And here all day they rise;
I seek the treasure of Thy love,
And close at hand it lies.

And a new song is in my mouth,
To long-loved music set,
Glory to Thee for all the grace
I have not tasted yet.

Anna L. Waring.

PRAYER

O Lord, that I might be God-centred in every way - God-centred in thought and word and deed, and not distracted from that centre. Bless us all today, garrison minds and hearts from vague fancies and inordinate affections, and from false emotions and spectres of the imagination, and keep us wholesomely Thine. Amen.

(Oswald Chambers).

TWENTY-SIXTH DAY

Read: 1 John 3:1-14

LIVING THE ABIDING LIFE.

"*Whosoever abideth in him sinneth not:* (does not go on sinning) *whosoever sinneth hath not seen him, neither known him.*"

v.6.

You will not find Sinless Perfection in this letter of the apostle John, but you do read much about Christian perfection. The idea that a Christian must inevitably sin while still in the flesh is not taught in scripture. Neither does the Bible teach that we can in this life get to a place where it is impossible to sin! To say it is possible not to sin is not the same as saying, it is impossible to sin!

John says in chapter 1:10 "*If we say we have no sin* (*have not sinned* Amp. Bible) *we deceive ourselves.*" Yet he goes on to say, "*These things write I unto you that ye sin not.*" (ch.2:1). A Christian who is walking in the light does not sin, so long as he is continuing to walk in the light. Whenever we do sin it is because we have not continued to walk in the light, ceased to abide in Christ. "*If we walk in the light*", says John "*as he is in the light, we have fellowship one with another, and the blood of Jesus Christ cleanses us from all sin.*" 1 John 1:7. I like that ancient prayer for purity, which begins, "*Almighty God, unto whom all hearts be open*". (We will use this prayer today.) We have this thought of being kept from sin also in the Te Deum, "*Vouchsafe, O Lord, to keep us this day without sin.*"

This is the teaching also of the apostle Paul in Romans chapters 6, 7 and 8. When you read Romans 6 you should note these words: In verse 6, "*knowing*"; v.11, "*reckon*"; v.13, "*yield*"; then we can come into the experience of v.18, "*Being made <u>free from sin</u> ye became* *the servants of righteousness.*" How could you sin while abiding in Jesus! The primary sin is to fail to abide in Him. But, thank God, confession always brings cleansing!

I want, dear Lord, a heart that's true and clean;
A sunlit heart, with not a cloud between,
A heart like Thine, a heart divine,
A heart as white as snow;
On me, dear Lord, a heart like this bestow.

I want, dear Lord, a love that feels for all;
A deep strong love that answers every call,
A love like Thine, a love divine,
A love for high and low;
On me, dear Lord, a love like this bestow.

I want, dear Lord, a soul on fire for Thee;
A soul baptized with heavenly energy.
A willing mind, a ready hand,
To do what-e'er I know,
To spread Thy light wherever I may go.

G. Jackson.

PRAYER

Almighty God, unto whom all hearts are open, all desires known, and from whom no secrets are hid; cleanse the thoughts of our hearts by the inspiration of Thy Holy Spirit, that we may perfectly love Thee, and worthily magnify Thy holy Name; through Jesus Christ our Lord. Amen.

(Book of Common Prayer).

The Lord's Prayer

TWENTY-SEVENTH DAY

Read: 1 John 3:15-24

LIVING THE ABIDING LIFE.

"Hereby we know that he abideth in us, by the Spirit which he hath given us." v.24.

A Christian is *'Born of the Spirit'* John 3:8, and is *'Sealed with the Spirit'* Eph. 1:13. Has been made a member of the body of Christ - the Church - *'by the Spirit'*, 1 Cor. 12:13. *"By one Spirit are we all baptized into one body"*. Note also, *"If any man have not the Spirit of Christ he is none of his."* Romans 8:9. And in 1 Cor. 12:3 we read, *"No man can say Jesus is Lord but by the Holy Ghost."* It is the Holy Spirit too who bears witness with our spirit that we are the children of God, see Romans 8:16, especially the R.V. Christians are exhorted to be *"Filled with the Spirit"* Eph. 5:18. To *"walk in the Spirit"* Gal. 5:16. To seek to manifest the *"fruit of the Spirit"* Gal. 5:22-25. So you see, Scripture has quite a lot to say about today's verse 1 John 3:24. We see better its full meaning by reading this verse in the Amplified Bible, so here it is: *"All who keep His commandments* (who obey His orders and follow His plan, live and continue to live, to stay) *abide in Him, and He in them. They let Christ be a home to them, and they are a home to Christ. And by this we know and understand and have the proof that He* (really) *lives and makes His home in us, by the* (Holy) *Spirit Whom He has given us."*

You may need to think carefully through all that, but it is helpful in that it gives us a full description of what it really means to live daily *'abiding in Christ'*. Let this teaching sink deeply into your heart. The Holy Spirit dwells within us, and the more we make room for Him so the more will He fill our lives. It is in this way that God leads His children on to maturity. We must live in daily dependence upon the indwelling of

God's Holy Spirit. It will be faith every step of the way; we came to know Christ by faith, and spiritual life is maintained daily by faith in Him so that as John tells us: *"Hereby we know that He abideth in us, by the Spirit which He hath given us"*.

Jesus, Thou joy of loving hearts,
Thou Fount of Life, Thou Light of men,
From the best bliss that earth imparts,
We turn unfilled to Thee again.

We taste Thee, O Thou Living Bread,
And long to feast upon Thee still;
We drink of Thee, the Fountain-head,
And thirst our souls from Thee to fill.

Our restless spirits yearn for Thee,
Where'er our changeful lot is cast;
Glad, when Thy gracious smile we see;
Blest, when our faith can hold Thee fast.

O Jesus, ever with us stay,
Make all our moments calm and bright;
Chase the dark night of sin away;
Shed o'er the world Thy holy light.

Latin 11th cent.
tr. Ray Palmer
(1808-1887).

PRAYER

The Lord's Prayer.

Almighty God, I thank Thee for the indwelling of Thy gracious Holy Spirit. I go forward into the day depending upon Thee, may Thy life be lived out through me to the praise of Thy glory. Amen.

TWENTY-EIGHTH DAY

Read: 2 Timothy 4:1-8

LIVING THE ABIDING LIFE.

"I have fought a good fight,
I have finished my course,
I have kept the faith."
v.7.

If we want an illustration of what it means in practical terms to live abiding in Christ, then we surely have it in the life of the apostle Paul. At the close of his earthly course he was able to look back and make this wonderful declaration to Timothy. Let me give this to you from the Amplified Bible: *"For I am already about to be sacrificed - my life is to be poured out* (as a drink offering); *the time for my* (spirit's) *release* (from the body) *is at hand and I will soon go free. I have fought the good* (worthy, honourable and noble) *fight; I have finished the race; I have kept* (firmly held) *the faith.* (As to what remains,) *henceforth there is laid up for me the* (victor's) *crown of righteousness - for being right with God and doing right - which the Lord, the righteous judge, will award to me and recompense me on that* (great) *day; and not to me only but also to all those who have loved and yearned for and welcomed His appearing* (His return)." v.6-8. *

The apostle Paul in spite of all his persecutions and suffering for the Gospel's sake had remained loyal to the truth and faithful to his Lord. He had closely followed the footsteps of the Master, and now in confident expectation he looks forward to receiving the victors crown. This will be the reward of all who follow his example, so he says, *"Not to me only, but to all those who love His appearing."* Keep close to Jesus, give heed to His Word, seek by God's grace to live in such union with your Lord that there may never be a cloud between Him and your soul, and you too may share this confident hope. *"I have kept the faith"* simply means I have lived the abiding life!

Take time to be holy,
Speak oft with thy Lord,
Abide in Him always,
And feed on His Word,
Make friends of God's children;
Help those who are weak;
Forgetting in nothing
His blessing to seek.

Take time to be holy,
Let Him be thy Guide;
And run not before Him
Whatever betide;
In joy or in sorrow
Still follow thy Lord,
And, looking to Jesus,
Still trust in His Word.

William D. Longstaff,
(1822-1894).

PRAYER

O Lord, into Thy hands do I commit this day. Give me a watchful, humble and diligent spirit, that I may seek in all things Thy will and gladly perform it for the honour of Thy Name. Amen.

---

* Some friends have asked about the Amplified Bible. The value of this work is that it includes various phases of meaning from the original languages. It can be obtained from a Bible Book Shop.

TWENTY-NINTH DAY

Read: Romans 12.

LIVING THE ABIDING LIFE, THE KEY.

"MAINTAIN THE SPIRITUAL GLOW."

v.11.

This quotation comes from Dr. Moffatt's translation, the whole verse being: *"Never let your zeal flag; maintain the spiritual glow; serve the Lord."* I want to give you a few practical hints which will enable you to live constantly abiding. Here is the key - Maintain the spiritual glow! And this is how we can do just that.

1. Beware of fluctuating feelings.

It is never wise for a Christian to take too much notice of feelings. We are saved, not because we feel saved, but through the sovereign grace and love of God. You have been saved by grace through faith, and you must go on in faith; some days you will feel spiritual and prayerful, other days you may feel far from being a Christian at all. Thank God our salvation does not depend upon our feeling saved! It depends upon something (or I should say, Someone) more trustworthy than mere feelings. This depends on God, and HE changes not.

2. Remember to gather your daily manna.

The children of Israel had to go out every morning and gather the food which God provided. He gave, they gathered. And God has provided spiritual food for us in His written Word, we must gather enough for each day, and as we feed, our souls are nourished. This is one of the main purposes for the suggested Bible portion in our "Five Minutes Before You Start". Get a thought for the day, then think about it whenever you can, as you do this it will become spiritual food for your soul. Our bodies require food and so do our souls. Never neglect the Word of God or you will not be able to live the abiding life.

3. Prayer is conversation.

Prayer is much more than merely asking God for things we need, it is talking with God, not only to Him. Two people engage in conversation: one speaks while the other one listens, then the first one listens while the other speaks. Practice being silent when you have prayed to God, HE may have something to say to you! As we wait in His divine presence the Lord can speak inwardly to our hearts. He can make known to us what His will may be. This is very important.

4. A set time for prayer is good, but it is not enough. Our set times of devotion need to be followed by talking to God through the day. Talk to Him as you would to a friend, about your work, your witness, your joys and sorrows. Eph. 6:18 "*Always*".

5. As soon as you are convicted - confess.

If you have done something wrong, confess it to God, as soon as you are convicted, and ask His forgiveness. Read 1 John 1:9. Note God's great promise in this verse, and always thank Him for His answer to your prayer.

PRAYER

Make this verse your prayer.

Lord, teach me how to pray aright,
With reverence and with fear;
Though dust and ashes in Thy sight,
I may, I must draw near.

James Montgomery.

THIRTIETH DAY

Read: Psalm 139

"Search me, O God, and know my heart: try me, and know my thoughts: and see if there be any wicked way in me, and lead me in the way everlasting."

v.23-24.

This must ever be our attitude in God's presence, *"Search me, O God"*. No morbid introspection caused by centring our thoughts upon ourselves as we try to see if we have sinned. Rather, may we have a humble openness toward God, letting His Holy Spirit convict us of any sin. If He does so then we must repent and seek His forgiveness. Always be ready to co-operate with God in His plan for your life; read good books to help you grow in grace. Beware of things about you in this world which could hinder your progress in a life of holiness.

Take note of the apostle's words as he writes to the Philippians 2:12 & 13, *"Work out your own salvation with fear and trembling; for it is God which worketh in you both to will and to do of His good pleasure."* The will to do comes from God, He also gives us the power to do His will. Jesus Christ is the *"Author and the finisher of our faith"* we read in Hebrews 12:2. Our faith originates with Him, and it will be brought to perfection by Him. Seek to live one day at a time: no, live one moment at a time. We must always draw upon the supplies of grace to be found in the Lord Jesus. We must let Him search our hearts and try our ways, and reveal to ourselves just where we stand in the light of His Word and will.

It is said that on one occasion, when Dr. F. B. Meyer was staying in the home of the Evangelist, D. L. Moody, that another evangelist, Dr. Wilbur Chapman shared with F. B. Meyer the fact that sometimes he felt full of power and yet at other times it was as though he had none. Dr. Meyer turned to him and said,

"Have you ever tried to breathe out three times whilst only breathing in once?" Think over that statement, there is a lot of instruction in it; then apply what you learn to your spiritual experience.

Search me, O God! my actions try
And let my life appear
As seen by Thine all-searching eye,
To mine my ways make clear.

Search all my sense and know my heart,
Who only canst make known
And let the deep, the hidden part
To me be fully shown.

Throw light into the darkened cells
Where passion reigns within;
Quicken my conscience till it feels
The loathsomeness of sin.

Search all my thoughts, the secret springs,
The motives that control;
The chambers where polluted things
Hold empire o'er the soul.

Search, till Thy fiery glance has cast
Its holy light through all
And I by grace am brought at last
Before Thy face to fall.

Francis Bottome,
(1823-1894).

PRAYER

The Lord's Prayer.

Heavenly Father grant me such grace that I may see my faults in the light of Thy holiness; and work in me to will and to do of Thy good pleasure. Amen.

SECTION ELEVEN

FIRST DAY

Read: Matt. 6:5-8 & 7:7-8

"But when you pray go into your room and shut the door and pray to your Father who sees in secret; and your Father who sees in secret shall reward you."

v.6.

This morning I received a letter from a former member of my church who reads these little messages, and he very kindly enclosed these helpful verses which will make a good start to this section.

TAKE TIME TO PRAY

"I got up early one morning
And rushed right into the day;
I had so much to accomplish
That I didn't have time to pray.
Problems came tumbling about me,
And heavier came each task;
"Why doesn't God help me?" I wondered:
He answered, "You didn't ask."

I wanted to see joy and beauty,
But the day toiled on, grey and bleak;
I wondered why God didn't show me:
He said, "You didn't seek."

I tried to come into God's presence,
I used all my keys at the lock:
God kindly and lovingly chided,
"My child, you didn't knock."

I woke up early this morning,
And paused before entering the day;
I had so much to accomplish
That I had to take time to pray.

Addie Dodds (U.S.A.)

Those verses are so true to experience you will not need me to elaborate further. We all know, only too well, their truth. I feel sure we grow in our appreciation of the Quiet Time as we realize, in ever increasing measure, its infinite value. For very many years I have made use of Oswald Chambers' Little Book of Prayers. It has now been entitled, 'Knocking at God's Door', and in the Foreword the Rev. David Lambert writes: "In this little book of prayers we are overhearing one of God's servants at prayer. These are some prayers that he breathed out to God, penning the very words in the exactness of his intention, in everything by prayer and supplication with thanksgiving to let his requests be made known unto God. They can teach us much about the simplicity, the range, the power and the perseverance of Spirit-born praying, and there is no service more worthy of our deepest attention." It would be well worth obtaining a copy of this little book of prayers, published by Marshall, Morgan Scott. Order from C.L.C. or any Bible Book Shop. 'Knocking at God's Door'.

Alone with God to hear what He shall say,
To seek from Him the manna for the day;
O loving Saviour, this is all my plea -
To follow on, and to know more of Thee.

Alone with God: to listen to His voice,
To know His will, and in that will rejoice;
To learn from Him the things He would impart -
Blest Spirit, now reveal them to my heart.

Alone with Him to feel His presence near:
What joy, what peace, what bliss beyond compare!
And all who love Him may the blessing share.

PRAYER

Almighty God, what a privilege it is for me to speak with Thee. Teach me more of what it means to really pray. Amen.

SECOND DAY

Read: Luke 10:38-42

"Martha, Martha, you are anxious and troubled about many things....." v.41.
"Mary hath chosen....." v.42.

This Mary-Martha story has been well called, The tale of two sisters. I am afraid sometimes Martha has been dealt with too harshly. It is possible for us to compare these two sisters and think of Mary as the good one, sitting at Jesus' feet, and Martha as the bad one, flustered and anxious. But if we look at this story a little more closely we see that they both had been listening to the words of Jesus. You will note it says it was Martha who received Jesus into her house; and verse 39 in the A.V. says: *"And she had a sister called Mary who also sat at Jesus' feet and heard his word."* So they both sat at Jesus' feet and heard his word. Yet so often the impression given is that Martha was only bothered about other things. The fact is that yielding to the dictates of her practical mind, Martha went to get on with other things; possibly to go and prepare a meal for them all. After a while, seeing her sister still sitting there while she was doing all the work, Martha became anxious and bothered by the fact that it was all being left for her to do. *"Cumbered about much serving"* is the way it is put in the A.V. It means she was distracted. She allowed material things to distract her from giving ear to what her Lord was saying. Oh, what a lovely human story this is! Martha waited for a while, then she blurted out, *"Lord, don't you care that my sister has left me to serve alone?"* Our Lord's reply was designed to help Martha get balance, to get the right perspective, as we say. Perhaps a little longer at the feet of Jesus and Martha would have been fortified against the distractions which resulted in her fretfulness, and her irritability with her sister. Things got so much on top of her that she even rebuked Jesus: *"Don't you care?"* What an awful thing to have done! I feel sure she did not realize what she had done by speaking to Jesus like that. Are you *'cumbered about much serving'?* It is so easy to fall into the trap.

Speak, Lord, in the stillness
While I wait on Thee;
Hush'd my heart to listen
In expectancy.

Speak, O Blessed Master,
In this quiet hour;
Let me see Thy face, Lord,
Feel Thy touch of power.

For the words Thou speakest,
"They are life indeed";
Living bread from heaven,
Now my spirit feed!

All to Thee is yielded,
I am not my own;
Blissful, glad surrender -
I am Thine alone.

Fill me with the knowledge
Of Thy perfect will;
All Thine own good pleasure
In Thy child fulfil.

E. May Grimes,
(1868-1927).

PRAYER

"O Lord, how essentially necessary it is for me to draw nigh to Thee. How can I falter when Thou art my life?".

Oswald Chambers.

THIRD DAY

Read: Psalm 119:1-8 and
Luke 10:38-42.
(Yes, read this again!)

"Mary hath chosen that good part, which shall not be taken away from her."

v.42.

"Mary hath chosen." I feel the right way to look at this story is to see that in each one of us there is this 'Mary spirit', that wants to sit at Jesus' feet, and also the 'Martha spirit' which may arise in conflict and cause us to become bogged down by material concerns. Often we have to pull ourselves up and listen afresh to these words of the Lord Jesus, *"Mary hath chosen that good part"*. It is so very easy to allow temporal matters to occupy too much of our time. I do not see that Jesus was condemning Martha for attending to their physical needs. Someone had to do the work! Where she went wrong was in becoming so over-burdened by the material things so that she lost out spiritually. Then of course, in her mind her sister was in the wrong. But really Martha was not in a fit state of mind to make a right judgment. It is so easy for us all to lose sight of the spiritual when we are so anxious about the temporal things of life. Our Lord's teaching on this matter was, *"Take no thought* (that is anxious thought) *for the morrow. Seek ye first the kingdom of God, and his righteousness, and all these things shall be added....."* Matt. 6:33.

It is not always easy to strike a right balance in these matters. I have just been reading some of the prayers in that little book to which I made reference the day before yesterday, and here is one of O.C.s prayers:

"Lord, how I realize the peril of work and activity equally with that of quiet retirement, and the only secure haven is Thyself. Help me to be taken up altogether with Thee."

Oh, how essential it is for us as Christian believers to keep a balance at all times between the passive and the active. Prayer and labour, faith and work, a restful assurance, and yet a constant dependence upon God. *"Mary hath chosen that good part which shall not be taken from her."*

Art thou hungering for the fulness
Of the blessing Christ doth give?
Longing now to learn the secret
Of the life He bids thee live?
In His Word thine answer standeth,
"Christ who is our Life" it saith;
Open now thy heart, and trust Him
There to dwell, henceforth, by faith.

In Him dwelleth all God's fulness,
In Him thou art made complete;
Rise, and claim thy heavenly birthright,
Kneeling at thy Father's feet.
He will never disappoint thee,
Praise Him that the gift is thine;
Then go forth and live each moment
On sufficiency divine.

Lord, I come, and simply resting
On Thy faithful, changeless word,
I believe the blood doth cleanse us,
And that Christ is crowned Lord.
Grant henceforth a ceaseless outflow
Of Thy life and love through me;
Reaching those who sit in darkness,
Winning priceless souls to Thee.

F. H. Allen.

PRAYER

Blessed Lord Jesus, I sit at Thy feet to learn of Thee. Show me Thy will for me today. Now, Lord, I go forth to serve Thee by serving others. Amen.

FOURTH DAY

Read: Philippians 3:20-21 & 4:1-7

"We are citizens of Heaven; our outlook goes beyond this world to the hopeful expectation of the Saviour who shall come from heaven, the Lord Jesus Christ, He will change these wretched bodies of ours so that they resemble his own glorious body, by that power of his which makes him the master of everything that is. So, my brothers, whom I love and long for, my joy and my crown, do stand firmly in the Lord, and remember how much I love you."

Phil. 3:20-21.
J. B. Phillips.

What a thought! What a hope and expectation! We are citizens of Heaven. The hope of a Christian goes far beyond this short life on earth. Christ will even change this '*body of our humiliation*' and make it like His glorified body. Because this is so the apostle exhorts us to stand firmly in the Lord. You will notice by the first few verses of chapter 4 that this glorious hope must have a great effect upon how we live here and now. So Paul exhorts those two sisters who had a difference to make it up. If you have a copy of J. B. Phillips New Testament it would help you to read these verses also. As you do note Paul says: *"Delight yourself in the Lord. Find your joy in Him at all times. And don't worry over anything whatever; tell God every detail of your needs in earnest thankful prayer, and the peace of God which transcends human understanding, will keep constant guard over your hearts and minds as they rest in Christ Jesus."*

There are some folk who never worry about anything, but they are certainly in the minority. It may be they have a fatalistic view of life, "What is to be will be", so why worry about it when you cannot change things. That attitude to life is far inferior to a positive trust in God that Paul exhorts us to have. A Christian has this privilege of taking everything to God in prayer, and through faith in the grace and power of the Lord frets and fears are replaced by the knowledge of God's neverfailing love so that we can experience what Paul calls the *'peace of God that passes all understanding'*. This is how the Lord would have us live this day and every day. Sheltered from the storms of life.

We bless Thee for Thy peace, O God,
Deep as the unfathomed sea,
Which falls like sunshine on the road
Of those who trust in Thee.

We ask not, Father, for repose
Which comes from outward rest,
If we may have through all life's woes
Thy peace within our breast.

That peace which suffers and is strong,
Trusts where it cannot see,
Deems not the trial-way too long,
But leaves the end with Thee;

That peace which flows serene and deep,
A river in the soul
Whose banks a living verdure keep,
God's sunshine o'er the whole.

Anon.

PRAYER

O Father, give my heart this peace,
Whate'er the outward be,
Till all life's discipline shall cease
And I come home to Thee.

Amen.

FIFTH DAY

Read: 2 Cor. 6:14-18 & 7:1-7

"We were troubled on every side; without were fightings, within were fears. Nevertheless God, that comforteth those that are cast down, comforted us by the coming of Titus."

v.5 & 6.

"Nevertheless God" - What weight those two words carry! They make all the difference. Paul did not try to let folk think he was not troubled, he had many trials but he could say: *"I am exceeding joyful in all our tribulation"*. Who ever heard of people being joyful in their troubles? None could talk like that unless they are able to say, *"Nevertheless God"*. You see it makes all the difference if you are a truly born-again believer, because whatever happens God is with you. That is what is meant by this little phrase - *"Nevertheless God"*. The apostle tells us that *"God, who comforts the downcast - dispirited, dejected, discouraged, depressed - comforted us by the coming of Titus."* This young man who worked with Paul in his missionary enterprises had called on the apostle with good news that his rebuke to the church at Corinth had resulted in good, and that cheered Paul's heart in the midst of his many trials.

It is good to know that God is still on the throne. Other people may fail, but God cannot fail. There are times in our lives when we must cast ourselves upon this fact - *"Never-the-less GOD"*. Many things may be against us but if God be for us who can prevail against us. This is the teaching of Paul in Romans 8:31-39 where he says, *"We are more than conquerors through him that loved us."* The wonderful thing about all this is that we also can, and should know this experience as Paul knew it. God has all sorts of ways of bringing us into this blessed knowledge of *"never-the-less God"*. God comforted Paul by the coming of Titus. I write and send out from time to time, what I call a 'Good Cheer'

"So, why are you cast down, O soul of mine; I will again hope in God and will praise Him."

(Psalm 42:11.)

O Lamb of God, still keep me
Close to Thy wounded side;
'Tis only there in safety
And peace I can abide.

What foes and snares surround me,
What lusts and fears within;
The grace that sought and found me,
Alone can keep me clean.

'Tis only in Thee hiding
I feel myself secure;
Only in Thee abiding,
The conflict can endure.

Thine arm the victory gaineth
O'er every hateful foe;
Thy love my heart sustaineth
In all its care and woe.

Deck.

PRAYER

Blessed Lord, my God, I thank Thee for the comfort of knowing in times of trial and difficulty I am not left alone without Thine aid. Yes, Lord, I know that underneath are Thine everlasting arms upholding me, and so I go on in Thy strength. Amen.

SEVENTH DAY

Read: Ezekiel 47:1-9

"He measured.....and brought me through."
v.3 & 4.

This vision of the holy waters is one which never fails to hold my attention. I see in this passage of Scripture a picture of the way God is continually seeking to lead His children on in their Christian experience. Here we see various depths of living water into which the Lord can bring us. First in verse 3, *"He measured a thousand cubits, and brought me through the waters: and the waters were to the ancles."* Here I see the beginner in his Christian life, he is in the water if only just. Shall we say, paddling? Then, note, verse 4, *"Again he measured a thousand and brought me through the waters; and the waters were to the knees"*. Thank God when by His gracious measuring we come to the experience when the waters are to the knees, and we no longer neglect what the Salvation Army call "Knee drill" - when we discover the value of prayer. But read on in this verse and you will see, *"Again he measured.....and brought me through: the waters were to the loins."* The loins the place of strength; here is a Christian with 'backbone'. But read on, verse 5, and note we have a further vision of God's purposes for us, namely, *"Waters to swim in."* Surely that is where the Lord is seeking to bring His children, to that place of spiritual freedom and we get our feet off the bottom, as it were, and enjoy the things of the Spirit which we could never know if we only paddle about in this river of God's life and power. I think the more you consider this the more you will enjoy this portion of God's Word, but it is this little phrase, *"He measured and brought me through"*, that I really want to share.

Some weeks ago I wrote to a Christian friend with whom I had not corresponded for some while. In fact this person kept coming to my mind so I prayed especially for her and sent a copy of my booklet, "When waves swamp the boat". In her reply she said, she had been going through similar experiences to those I relate in the book, and that she had experienced the strength of God as He often sustained her through verses of Scripture. Then she said, one Scripture which had been a great help was this verse I have selected for you today: *"He measured and brought me through"*. That was this sister's testimony. Yes, praise God, He is always measuring and bringing us through; and what a patient Leader! God will bring you through your present trial, and into a greater experience of His love - *"waters to swim in"*. Bless the Lord!

O Pilgrim bound for the heavenly land,
Never lose sight of Jesus!
He'll lead you gently with loving hand:
Never lose sight of Jesus!

Never lose sight of Jesus!
Never lose sight of Jesus!
Day and night He will lead you right:
Never lose sight of Jesus!

When you are tempted to go astray,
Never lose sight of Jesus!
Press onward, upward the narrow way;
Never lose sight of Jesus!

Rev. Johnson Oatman.

PRAYER

Blessed Saviour, I thank Thee that Thou wilt bring me through and so I look afresh to Thee. Amen.

The Lord's Prayer.

EIGHTH DAY

Read: 2 Cor. 5:17, 6:10

"We then, as workers together with him."
ch. 6:1.

"Workers together" - That phrase caught my eye this morning, and I thought of all those who are now regular readers of these little Bible messages. One of the happy, yet quite unexpected features of this ministry, is that we receive so many encouraging letters. As many of these books are passed on by readers to their friends, there is now quite a Fellowship of F.M.B.Y.S. (as some call the books). I would like to say that our text for today seems most appropriate, because although I write these and my wife does a lot of the work entailed in producing them, our circulation has grown naturally by readers recommending them to other folk so that more and more orders are received. I would like to give you one or two extracts from letters, as these will show just what I mean. "Thank you for sending the books I ordered, they came in time for distribution to my ladies. Today is the first time I have seen my ladies since giving out their gifts, and three of them testified to the blessing they received by reading their 'lovely book'. So we praise God....." Mrs. M. W., Humberside. "Please would you send me 2 copies 'Praying in our Prayers' as it has been a real blessing to me over the years. Also 2 'When waves swamp the boat', I had some but gave them away. I want to give a 'Praying in our Prayers' to a lady I visit." - Miss D. B., London. "I am so enjoying your 'No. 10'. It seems to fit every occasion." - Mrs. D. M., Sussex. "I have two friends who are young in the Christian faith, I wish to encourage them to read the Holy Bible regularly. One I led to the Lord Jesus when he was in the same ward while I was in hospital." - Mr. M. C., Surrey.

So you see what I mean by our being, "*Workers together*". Christians are, "*New creatures in Christ*", we have just read, and as such we are "*workers together with HIM*". When you pray each day would you please pray for all others who are reading these messages, in that way we surely can help one another. Thank you for all your prayers for us as we prepare these. Now read ch. 6:10 again and note those divine paradoxes!

Make use of me, my God,
Let me not be forgot;
A broken vessel cast aside,
One whom Thou neededest not.

I am Thy creature, Lord,
Made by hands divine;
And I am part, however mean,
Of this great world of Thine.

Thou usest all Thy works,
The weakest things that be;
Each has a service of its own,
For all things wait on Thee.

All things do serve Thee here,
All creatures great and small;
Make use of me, of me, my God,
The meanest of them all.

Horatius Bonar,
(1808-1889).

PRAYER

Almighty God, what a privilege that I am a worker together with Thee, and with other believers. Lord, show me how I can work with Thee today. Amen.

NINTH DAY

Read: Isaiah 30:15-21

"For thus saith the Lord God, the Holy One of Israel, In returning and rest ye shall be saved; in quietness and in confidence shall be your strength." v.15.

As I have been praying and waiting on the Lord this morning, this word has come to me with that quiet certainty that marks it out as God's message for me just now. Many of you will know what I mean by that: it is in such a way that God speaks to us, as He re-speaks the Words of Scripture into our hearts and applies it to our present need. When I was a young Christian I read a book about Bible Marking and found it very helpful. The Bible is such a big book and to underline some verse which may have been a help can make it easier to find when you want it another time. As I turned to this book of Isaiah these verses chosen as our reading for today stood out because in addition to verses 15, 18 and 19, being underlined in red, the whole portion down to verse 21 is sectioned off by a blue vertical line in the margin.

What a world of clamour we live in these days! Over the air by radio and television is poured forth much that serves as noisy distractions. Cars, lorries, juggernauts, not only belch out their pollution into the air, but they all send forth their contribution of incessant noise. Those of us who live in the quiet places of the earth have more to be thankful for than we realize. Yet, you know, there can be peace all around and turmoil in the heart. God says, *"In returning and rest ye shall be saved; in quietness and in confidence shall be your strength."* Note the two things God says to His children: *"In returning and rest ye shall be saved"*. Have you been getting a little bit slack, and away from God lately? Here is God's loving call to return! *"In quietness and in confidence shall be your strength"*. Here is God's gracious call to troubled hearts! Have you found a restless spirit take hold of you so that you feel more at home amid noise and rush of worldly things, than in the quietness of God's presence? Then notice this: confidence grows out of the quietness. *"Speak, Lord, in the stillness while I wait on Thee."* Now so far you will see I have omitted the last four words in verse 15. They are such sad words - *"but ye would not"*. Oh, how much may be lost if we will not obey God's call! Yes, but what a lot can be gained by heeding His call! *"In quietness and in confidence shall be YOUR strength."*

O walk with Jesus, wouldst thou know
How deep, how wide His love can flow!
They only fail His love to prove
Who in the way of sinners rove.

Walk thou with Him; that way is light,
All other pathways end in night;
Walk thou with Him; that way is rest,
All other pathways are unblest.

O walk with Jesus! to thy view
He will make all things sweet and new;
Will bring new fragrance from each
flower,
And hallow every passing hour.

Edwin Paxton Hood,
(1820-1885)

PRAYER

Blessed Lord, my God, I return to Thee for Thou alone canst meet my need. Keep me in the centre of Thy will. Amen.

TENTH DAY

Read: John 1:1-17

"And of His fulness have all we received, and grace for grace."
v.16.

I thought, for the next three weeks it would be good for us to meditate upon some of the teachings of this Gospel of John. I only select a few verses, and can write but briefly about one each day; but it can bring you much blessing if sometime during each day you can read the rest of the chapter. You will then have read the whole of this Gospel in just three weeks.

Today, I am thinking about that little phrase in verse 16: *"Grace for grace"*. Note first, John brings to us the great and fundamental truth that the Lord Jesus Christ, Whom he calls, *"The Word"* in v.1 is none other than divine. *"The Word was with God and the Word was God."* Then as we read only down to verse 12 John tells us the purpose of His coming into this world. Read that verse again now, and see that this is how we become children of God. In this *verse 16* John is addressing those who have received Christ as Saviour and Lord, and he says: *"Of His fulness have all we received"*, it is of that full and divine life that we have received when we received Jesus. Then he goes on to say, *"and grace for grace"*. These words always intrigued me although I was not sure of their exact meaning until I read in one of Amy Carmichael's books where she quotes from Bishop Moule's explanation of this passage. He says: *"Grace for grace"* - the word *'for'* in this verse simply means *'instead'*. The image is of a perpetual succession of supply; a displacement ever going on; ceaseless changes of need and demand. "The picture before us is as of a river. Stand on its banks, and contemplate the flow of waters. A minute passes, and another. Is it the same stream still? Yes. But is it the same water? No. The liquid mass that passed you a few seconds ago, now fills another section of the channel; new water has displaced it, or if you please replaced it; water instead of water. And so hour by hour, year by year, century by century, the process holds. One stream, other waters, living not stagnant, because always there is perpetual exchange. Grace takes the place of grace; love takes the place of love, on and on, hour after hour, year after year - a perpetual supply of God's grace through Christ." Isn't that lovely! Let its truth grip you.

Grace, 'tis a charming sound,
Harmonious to the ear;
Heaven with the echo shall resound,
And all the earth shall hear.

Grace first contrived a way
To save rebellious man;
And all the steps that grace display
Which drew the wondrous plan.

Grace taught my wandering feet
To tread the heavenly road;
And new supplies each hour I meet,
While pressing on to God.

Philip Doddridge,
(1702-1751).

PRAYER

Almighty God, I praise and worship Thee for Thy love and grace made known in Christ Jesus; for grace that saves and for grace that keeps. Amen.

ELEVENTH DAY

Read: John 2:1-11

"Jesus and his disciples were called (invited) *to the wedding."* v.2.

"And manifested forth his glory". v.10.

This was, we are told, the first miracle Jesus did. The last was when He healed the ear of the soldier which Peter had slashed in the garden on the night of the betrayal. *"Jesus.....was invited to the wedding"*, and what a difference it made! It always does. I have attended and conducted very many weddings, and oh, what a difference, what a contrast there often is between a wedding of practising Christians and that of those who do not know the Lord, although for some reason or other want to be married in church. There seems to be a completely different atmosphere. The singing is different, the responses are different even although the words are the same. The reception is different. Yes, let me repeat, it makes all the difference when Jesus is invited to the wedding, when He lives in the hearts of the happy couple and transforms their home! Things could have gone very wrong at that wedding in Cana had not the Lord Jesus been there. *"The mother of Jesus saith unto him, They have no wine."* His reply as we read it in our A.V. sounds hard to our ears, but really He addressed His mother using a term of endearment, Dear woman.....(see Amplified Bible). Now I want you to notice that this miracle was made possible by the obedience of the servants. Jesus said, *"Fill the waterpots with water"*, and *"they filled them to the brim"*. Our Lord's mother had said to them, *"Whatsoever he saith unto you, do it."* v.5. If you now read that phrase over four times, each time placing the emphasis on the words I will underline, you will discover truths that lie hidden in its depths. *"Whatsoever He saith unto you do it."* *"Whatsoever HE....."* *"Whatsoever He saith unto you....."* *"Whatsoever He saith unto you do it.*" You see, the first shows the extent of our obedience. The second emphasises the greatness of Him who commands us. The third, applies what He is saying to ourselves. The fourth, is a command in two words - "*do it*". May we be given grace so to do. He will only ask us to do what we can do - "*fill the waterpots*", HE does the rest. And note the result: "*He manifested forth His glory.*" v.10.

O Father all creating,
Whose wisdom, love and power
First bound two lives together
In Eden's primal hour;
Today to these Thy children
Thine earliest gifts renew;
A home by Thee made happy,
A love by Thee kept true.

O Saviour, Guest most bounteous
Of old in Galilee,
Vouchsafe today Thy presence,
With these who call on Thee;
Their store of earthly gladness
Transform to heavenly wine,
And teach them in the tasting,
To know the gift is Thine.

John Ellerton.

PRAYER

O God, grant me Thy grace that I may know what Thou wouldst have me do, and Thy strength to do it at all times. Amen.

TWELFTH DAY

Read: John 3:1-16

"That which is born of the flesh is flesh; and that which is born of the Spirit is spirit. Marvel not that I said unto thee, Ye must be born again (from above)".

v. 6 & 7.

John 3:16 has been called "The Gospel in a nutshell". Here we have the very kernel of truth, and this verse divides up into two parts: God's part and ours. *"God so loved that He gave....."* and *"Whosoever believeth....."*. It may be said that here divine sovereignty and human responsibility meet. Notice those little words in v.14. *"As....."*, *"So....."*. The brazen serpent was a type of the cross of Jesus. Just as people were saved from the effects of the snake bites, by the obedience of faith, when they looked to the serpent on the pole in Moses' day so are we saved from Satan's power by looking in faith to the Lord Jesus.

"Whosoever believeth in him should not perish, but have everlasting life." v.15. Thus are we 'born again', born into God's family through faith in Christ. *"Ye must be born again"*, means 'from above'. We all need this spiritual new birth. It is not easy to explain but we can experience this through God's grace. Let me give you verse 8 from J. B. Phillips: "The wind blows where it likes, you can hear the sound of it but you have no idea where it comes from and where it goes. Nor can you tell how a man is born by the wind of the Spirit." You cannot see the wind, but you can certainly feel its affect. You cannot see it, but you can see what it does. We thank God for the transforming power of God's Spirit which can make us *"new creatures in Christ Jesus."* 2 Cor. 5:17. So the apostle Peter says, *"As new born babes desire the sincere milk of the word that ye may grow thereby."* 1 Peter 2:2. Often this growth is like that of a

tulip bulb, there is the unseen work of inward growth which causes the bulb to shoot, then there is the steady and silent growth day by day until the beauty of the full bloom is seen and can be enjoyed. God's work in our souls is often a steady, silent work of grace. Peter tells us that we *"Grow in grace as we grow in the knowledge of our Lord and Saviour Jesus Christ."* See 2 Peter 3:18.

A Ruler once came to Jesus by night,
To ask Him the way of salvation and light;
The Master made answer in words true and plain,
"Ye must be born again".

"Ye must be born again," (repeat)
I verily, verily, say unto you -
"Ye must be born again!"

Ye children of men, attend to the word
So solemnly uttered by Jesus the Lord,
And let not this message to you be in vain,
"Ye must be born again".

W. T. Sleeper.

PRAYER

Blessed Lord Jesus, make me a true child of God. Take from my heart all that grieves Thee, and fill me with Thy Holy Spirit that I may live for Thee. Amen.

The Lord's Prayer

THIRTEENTH DAY

Read: John 4:1-14

"Jesus said, Whosoever drinketh of this water shall thirst again: but whosoever drinketh of the water that I shall give him shall never thirst; but the water that I shall give him shall be in him a well of water springing up into everlasting life."
v. 13/14.

Outside Holy Trinity Church in Robertson Street, near the sea front here at Hastings there is a red granite drinking fountain, and these words of the Lord Jesus have been engraved on it. As I was reading them one day I suddenly realized it would be no use if someone parched with thirst came to that fountain for a drink, it is very obvious that it has been out of commission for a long time now. A fountain but no water! I have no doubt when it was erected during the Victorian era it was connected to the supply of drinking water. I am sure there must have been many a traveller in days gone by who came thirsty to that fountain and by pressing the button had released a steady flow of clear, refreshing water, and left that spot feeling much better for the water he had received freely. As I looked at those familiar words taken from this Gospel, I wondered how many souls had read them and realized their spiritual meaning. It is quite possible that even today, although that particular fountain is dry, the words of the Saviour inscribed thereon can speak to spiritually thirsty men and women. We cannot live without water; and so Jesus used this as an analogy of that spiritual life which thirsty souls can receive by receiving Him as personal Lord and Saviour. And although that fountain is dry, not so with Jesus! He says: *"The water that I shall give him shall be in him a well of water springing up into everlasting life."* Earthly fountains may fail but Jesus is the Lifegiving Fountain who will never fail to refresh thirsty souls, but remember it is thirsty souls Jesus can satisfy. He put it another way when He said, *"I came not to call the righteous, but sinners to repentance."* Read the whole story and see what a great difference Jesus made in the life of this woman, read verses 39-42 now.

I hunger and I thirst;
Jesus, my manna be;
Ye living waters burst
Out of the rock for me.

Thou bruised and broken Bread,
My lifelong wants supply;
As living souls are fed,
O feed me, or I die.

Thou true life-giving Vine,
Let me Thy sweetness prove;
Renew my life with Thine,
Refresh my soul with love.

For still the desert lies
My thirsting soul before;
O living waters, rise
Within me evermore.

John S. B. Monsell,
(1811-1875).

PRAYER

O Lord of all creation, I praise Thee that Thou hast supplied our need for spiritual refreshing. I thank Thee that all my fresh springs are in Thee; I come, and will keep coming to the Fountain of all goodness and my soul's deepest longings are satisfied. Amen.

FOURTEENTH DAY

Read: John 5:17-24

"Verily, verily, I say unto you, the Son can do nothing of himself, but what he seeth the Father do: for what things soever he doeth, these also doeth the Son likewise."

v.19.

"Verily, verily." You will find this affirmation three times in this chapter, v.19; 24; 25 and twenty-four times altogether in this Gospel. This is an interesting phrase: it is a confirmation to confirm a statement beyond all doubt. It means, truly, truly, I wish to assert that what I am saying can be relied upon; it is true, and sure, and irrefutable. So when you come to read those two words, notice with great care what follows for it will be an important statement. We will just now consider the three times this phrase is found in this chapter. First, here, v.19 *"Verily, verily...."* Read the verse again now. Here we see how Jesus was so much at one with the Father. What Jesus said and did was what the Father was saying and doing. That is what He meant in ch. 10:30. *"I and my Father are one"*. For this reason all men should honour the Son as they honour the Father, v.23 *"Ye believe in God, believe also in me."* 14:1. Then in v.24 *"Verily, verily, I say unto you, He that heareth my word, and believeth on him that sent me, hath everlasting life, and shall not come into condemnation; but is passed from death unto life."* This is, of course, in the spiritual sense. Read also John 3:36 here. Note too, *"Shall not come into condemnation"*. See John 3:18 and Romans 8:1. Then again in verse 25 *"Verily, verily, the hour is coming, and now is, when the dead shall hear* (those who are spiritually dead) *the voice of the Son of God: and they that hear shall live." "He that hath ears to hear - he who is ready to listen attentively - let him hear - and take note of what I am saying."* Matt. 13:9. It is in this way that we come out of darkness into light, out of

death into life, out of the kingdom of Satan into the kingdom of God's dear Son. See Colossians 1:12-14.

I hear the words of love,
I gaze upon the blood;
I see the mighty sacrifice,
And I have peace with God.

'Tis everlasting peace,
Sure as Jehovah's name;
'Tis stable as His steadfast throne,
For evermore the same.

The clouds may go and come,
And storms may sweep the sky,
This blood-sealed friendship changes not,
The cross is ever nigh.

I change, He changes not,
The Christ can never die;
His love, not mine, the resting place,
His truth, not mine the tie.

Horatius Bonar,
(1808-1889).

PRAYER

Almighty Father, I thank Thee for the Lord Jesus Christ, and that He ever did Thy holy will. Help me to listen to His words, and follow Him. Amen.

FIFTEENTH DAY

Read: John 6:41-58

Jesus said: *"I am the living bread which came down from heaven: if any man eat of this bread, he shall live for ever: and the bread that I will give is my flesh, which I will give for the life of the world."* v.51.

Manna from heaven, that is what sustained the Israelites all through their wilderness journey. *"Angels food"* the Psalmist called it, Psalm 78:24/25. But, of course, even manna, although it was God's provision for their bodies, could not give them everlasting life. So, says Jesus, *"I am that bread of life your fathers did eat manna in the wilderness and are dead. This is the bread that cometh down from heaven, that a man may eat thereof and not die."*

Of course, our Lord was giving spiritual teaching about the purpose of His coming, and declares that HE is living bread - life imparting bread, and believing in Him (see v.47) is like partaking of heavenly bread. To partake of eternal life we must become partakers of His life, which is eternal. He gives us His life by giving His body, His flesh, on Calvary's cross. If we will believe in Him, receive Him and abide in Him, we shall live for ever. How sad that some could only interpret what Jesus said in a material sense, and therefore complained, *"How can this man give us his flesh to eat?"* v.52. Truly such mysteries can only be revealed by the Father to 'babes' - simple, humble minded. See Matt. 11:26. It would be of little use to have a loaf of bread on the table to look at, if our bodies are to be sustained we need to eat it - receive it into ourselves. Just so in the spiritual realm, we need to eat - partake - of Christ the bread of life. Are we nourishing our souls on Christ? Are we daily receiving Him into our lives by receiving His word and by prayer and seeking to abide in His will?

This is what Jesus meant by receiving His body and blood. Some have seen in this passage an interpretation of the sacramental feast of bread and wine in Holy Communion. That does not figure in the context, but it is true that in a spiritual sense we do '*feed upon Christ with thanksgiving*' whenever we rightly partake of the bread and wine in grateful memory of Him.

Jesus, Thou joy of loving hearts,
Thou Fount of Life, Thou Light of men,
From the best bliss that earth imparts,
We turn unfilled to Thee again.

We taste Thee, O Thou Living Bread,
And long to feast upon Thee still;
We drink of Thee, the Fountain-head,
And thirst our souls from Thee to fill.

Our restless spirits yearn for Thee,
Where'er our changeful lot is cast;
Glad, when Thy gracious smile we see;
Blest, when our faith can hold Thee fast.

Latin 11th Cent.
tr. Ray Palmer,
(1808-1887).

PRAYER

"In confidence of Thy goodness and great mercy, O Lord, I draw near unto Thee, as a sick person to the Healer, as one hungry and thirsty to the Fountain of Life, a creature to the Creator, a desolate soul to my own tender Comforter. Amen."

- Thomas a Kempis.

SIXTEENTH DAY

Read: John 7:1-11 & 37-44

Jesus said: *"He that believeth on me, as the scripture hath said, out of his innermost being shall flow rivers of living water. But this spake he of the Spirit, which they that believe on him should receive."*

v.38 & 39.

It was the Feast of the Tabernacles, when the Jews left their houses and dwelt for eight days in tents, sometimes just shelters made from branches of trees. This was intended as a reminder of the time when they lived in tents in the wilderness, and it was a time of great rejoicing that God had brought them through those days to the land of promise. This was one of three of the Feasts of Jehovah when all the males among the Jews were obliged to attend, so there was a great concourse of people in Jerusalem. During those eight days the law was read and sacrifices made. The last day was called the Great day of the feast and in addition to the final reading of the law there was a special ceremony when the priests went to the pool of Siloam and brought back into the Temple water in a golden vial, this was poured out upon the sacrifice in front of all the people. We do not read of this in the Bible and it seems to be one of those many traditions which had grown up over the years. I want you to use your imagination a little here, and you will see what an impact the words of Jesus must have made upon many. With great ceremony and ritual we see the procession as they arrive in the Temple with this golden vial filled with water from the pool. With great solemnity they pour in a little wine, and then at a given moment while all eyes are upon him the priest lifts it above his head and pours the contents out over the sacrifice being offered. Listen, in the silence of that moment a loud voice is heard: *"If any man thirst, let him come unto me and drink. He that believeth on me as the scripture hath said, out of him shall flow rivers of living water."* It is the voice of the prophet of Galilee again! What consternation! John when writing explains in verse 39 *"This spake He of the Spirit, which they that believe on Him should receive."* Many consider that this is what happened. But note, THIRST. Are you thirsty? Come to Jesus and drink of His life-giving Spirit, and rivers will flow out to needy ones around you.

Rivers of living water,
Rivers that flow from the throne.
Rivers o'erflowing with blessing,
Coming from Jesus alone.

Rivers of living water,
Rivers of life so free,
Flowing from Thee my Saviour -
Send now the rivers thro' me.

Cleanse me, oh, cleanse me, my Saviour
Make me a channel to-day;
Empty me, fill me and use me,
Teach me to trust and obey.

G. R. H. Wood.

PRAYER

Blessed Saviour, I believe in Thee, and I am thirsty for Thy Spirit. Cleanse my heart, and fill me with Thy Spirit, that out from me Thy love may flow to others. Amen.

SEVENTEENTH DAY

Read: John 8:30-42

"Ye shall know the truth, and the truth shall make you free." "If therefore the Son shall make you free, ye shall be free indeed."

v.32 & 36.

"THE TRUTH SHALL MAKE YOU FREE." How sad that the re-action of some was, *"We were never in bondage."* (v.33). It is often this attitude to the teaching of Christ which stands in the way of men entering into that spiritual freedom which is God's design, and which Christ came to give. *"Made free?"* They said, *"We are not in bondage to any man."* So our Lord went on to demonstrate this awful fact, that they were actually slaves - slaves to sin. (It is the stronger word here, not just servants but slaves!) That is our basic problem. We are all slaves to sin until Christ sets us free. You can easily test the truth of that statement by considering the fact that there are some temptations to sin which you find difficult to overcome. You get the victory at one time, yet fall at another. Try as you may, you can't get free. It is an awful realization when we come to see how deep is our need. Sin is so much part of man's nature that without the power of Christ to set us free, we would for ever be in bondage to evil, and the evil one.

Here is a marvellous message! What we all need is deliverance; and what we all may have is DELIVERANCE! Deliverance from the guilt and the power of sin. Jesus did not die to make forgiveness possible, He died to secure forgiveness for all who will believe, and to make deliverance a practical reality for all who will believe. We are justified by faith, and we are sanctified by faith in His power to deliver. The truth shall make you free. So Paul says, *"Being made free from sin, ye became servants of righteousness."* Rom. 6:18. *"If the Son shall make you free, ye shall be free indeed."* I have many hundreds of sermon notes, and looking through some recently I came across this: Scriptural Freedom from Sin, as seen in Romans 6 v.6. *"Knowing";* v.11 *"Reckon";* v.13 *"Yield",* and the result - v.14 *"Sin shall not have lordship over you."* v.18 *"Made FREE".*

Free from the law, oh, happy condition!
Jesus hath died, and there is remission!
"Come unto Me", oh, hear His sweet call!
Grace hath redeemed us once for all.

Now are we free - there's no condemnation
Jesus provides a perfect salvation;
"Come unto Me", oh, hear His sweet call!
Come, and He saves us once for all.

"Children of God", oh, glorious calling!
Surely His grace will keep us from falling!
Passing from death to life at His call,
Blessed salvation once for all.

P. P. Bliss.

PRAYER

Almighty God, I praise Thy Name that Thou hast forgiven all my sin through Thy wonderful grace. Lord Jesus, Thou art my Saviour - Deliverer - and I yield my heart to Thee, Thou dost set me free. Amen.

EIGHTEENTH DAY

Read: John 9:1-25

"Give God the praise: we know that this man is a sinner. He answered and said, Whether he be a sinner or no I know not: one thing I know, that, whereas I was blind now I see."

v.25.

It will well repay you to read the whole of this chapter sometime to-day. Here we see a man whose appreciation of Jesus grew as his understanding of Him became more clear. First, when he received his sight, all he could say to those who wanted to know who it was that healed him: *"He was a man called Jesus"* v.11. Later the Pharisees said, *"This man is not of God"*, and that started an argument. When he was challenged as to what he thought about Jesus, this man said: *"He is a prophet"*. After he had been cast out of the synagogue (a terrible thing to happen to a Jew as that caused much persecution and privation). Jesus met him and said, *"Do you believe on the Son of God?"* The man replied, *"Who is he Lord, that I might believe on him?"* v.36. Jesus then revealed the truth concerning who He was, and the result was that he said, *"Lord, I believe. And he worshipped Jesus"* v.38.

Do you see here a gradual unfolding of truth to this man. First, the Saviour was "A *man called Jesus"*; then *"He is a prophet"* and finally, this restored man confessed the Lord Jesus as the Son of God and believed in Him and worshipped Him. Isn't that just what happens so often, gradually people come to see that the Jesus in the Christmas story is a prophet, and more than a prophet, The Son of the living God. It is then that we become worshippers of the Lord Jesus Christ. Other people may think of Him as an imposter, *"This man is not of God because he keepeth not the Sabbath day."* Some may say He is a sinner, but the person who once was spiritually blind and has now come to see who Jesus really is, will certainly believe in Him and worship Him. *"Once I was blind but now I can see, the Light of the world is Jesus."*

Lord, I was blind; I could not see
In Thy marred visage any grace,
But now the beauty of Thy face
In radiant vision dawns on me.

Lord, I was deaf; I could not hear
The thrilling music of Thy voice:
But now I hear Thee and rejoice,
And all Thy uttered words are dear!

Lord, I was dead; I could not stir
My lifeless soul to come to Thee:
But now, since Thou hast quickened me,
I rise from sin's dark sepulchre.

For Thou hast made the blind to see,
The deaf to hear, the dumb to speak,
The dead to live; and, lo, I break
The chains of my captivity.

William T. Matson,
(1833-1899).

PRAYER

Lord Jesus Christ, give me an ever increasing appreciation of Thy glorious Person. Thou art the Christ, the Son of the Living God. Amen.

Spend some time in worshipping the Lord just now. Praise Him for His own Person, and His work of redemption.

NINETEENTH DAY

Read: John 10:22-33

"My sheep hear my voice, and I know them, and they follow me; and I give unto them eternal life; and they shall never perish, neither shall any man pluck them out of my hand."

v.27 & 28.

Our Lord Jesus had been giving His parable about the sheep and the shepherd. He declared Himself to be *"The good shepherd that giveth his life for the sheep."* v.11. And said He, *"Other sheep I have which are not of this* (Jewish) *fold, them also I must bring, and they shall hear my voice; and there shall be one fold and one shepherd."* v.16. This was our Lord's prediction that the Gospel would be preached also to Gentiles. There shall be *'one fold'* ('one flock', J. N. Darby & others) and one Shepherd. The church of Christ is made up of both Jews and Gentiles who believe in Him. There is no distinction, *"Ye are all one in Christ Jesus"*. (See Gal. 3:27/28 & Eph. 2:14-18.) The sheep are those who *'hear His voice and follow Him'*. That is those who respond to the effectual call of God. *"I know them"*, says Jesus. Yes, *"the Lord knoweth them that are His."* 2 Tim. 2:19. Here is the test of true Christian experience, *"they follow me"* says the Good Shepherd. To follow Jesus means we follow His teachings and His way of life. They are people who do God's will and walk in God's ways, Micah 6:8. Of such Jesus says: *"I give unto them eternal life, and they shall never perish."* The final preservation of the believer, our eternal security, is clearly taught in this passage of Scripture. I feel sure that some who object to this truth, do so because they misunderstand what exactly is taught about it in God's Word. It certainly does not mean that anyone who has made a profession of belief in Christ without any change in their life can claim eternal security. We must follow through these two verses very carefully, when we do we will see that to be in the blessing of verse 28 we must be in the experience of verse 27. Read them over again and you will see how true this is. Read also 2 Peter 1:4-10.

Sovereign grace o'er sin abounding,
Ransomed souls the tidings swell;
'This a deep that knows no sounding;
Who its breadth or length can tell?
On its glories
Let my soul for ever dwell.

What from Christ that soul shall sever,
Bound by everlasting bands?
Once in Him, in Him for ever;
Thus the eternal covenant stands;
None shall pluck thee
From the strength of Israel's hands.

Heirs of God, joint-heirs with Jesus,
Long ere time its race begun;
To His name eternal praises;
Oh, what wonders He hath done!
One with Jesus
By eternal union one.

John Kent,
(1766-1843).

PRAYER

Almighty God, through faith in our Lord Jesus Christ I am one with Thee. I praise Thee that the grace that saves is also the grace that will keep me. Amen.

TWENTIETH DAY

Read: John 11:1-11 & 20-24

"Now Jesus loved Martha and her sister, and Lazarus. When he heard therefore that he was sick, he abode still two days in the same place where he was."

v.5 & 6.

What a mystery! Jesus loved these folk, yet when he heard of their distress He abode two days where He was. Why ever didn't Jesus hurry and go to them? One would think verse 6 would read, 'He hurried off to see them'. No, it does not say that! It is obvious that Jesus purposely delayed going to them, and yet He loved them! How could He hold back when their need was so great? *"Lord, if thou hadst been here, my brother would not have died."* said Martha in v.21. The reason they sent for Jesus was that He might prevent their brother from dying. (v.3.) What was the reason for our Lord's delay? If you read verse 4 again you will see more clearly that Jesus had a reason, and a very important one. *"This sickness is not unto death,* (its ultimate purpose is not the final departure of Lazarus) *but for the glory of God, that the Son of God might be glorified thereby."* Oh, so Jesus knew something that Mary and Martha did not know! Even the disciples could not understand what was His reason for the delay. (See v.11-13.)

Of course we have the complete story before us, we know now that Jesus wept at the tomb of His friend. We read now that Jesus challenged their faith by saying, *"Said I not unto thee, that, if thou wouldest believe, thou shouldest see the glory of God."* v.40. We know that Jesus cried with a loud voice, *"Lazarus come forth"*, and they saw Jesus the Victor over man's greatest enemy, death. But they did not know at the time, all they knew was that Jesus did not come as soon as He was sent for. It was a great mystery to these sisters, they only saw what had happened to their brother. Jesus saw what was going to happen to him. Jesus saw Lazarus alive again, and many of the people believing when they saw He was the Resurrection and the Life! Yes our Lord had a purpose in all that He allowed to happen. He always has! Don't you think there is a lesson for us all just here? *"What I do, thou knowest not now, but thou shalt know hereafter."* Faith believes in spite of all mysteries.

Give me, O Lord, a faith serene
That rests in Thee alone,
Assured that grace divine has made
Me all Thine own.

Teach me, O Lord, to understand
Even in the darkest night,
When storms are high and seas are wild
Thy way is right.

Upon me, Lord, Thy peace bestow
When foes assail my heart;
Appoint me some sweet meeting place
With Thee apart.

Grant me, O Lord, to feel Thy hand
Of tenderness and power
Is holding mine and leading me
Each day, each hour.

Norman R. Perry,
(1909-).

PRAYER

Blessed Lord, I praise Thee that Thou art with me always, and all the days. Amen.

TWENTY-FIRST DAY

Read: John 13:1-14

Jesus said to Peter, *"If I wash thee not thou hast no part with me."* (v.8).
"He that is washed (bathed) *needeth not save to wash his feet, but is clean every whit."* (v.10).

Let us look at this passage in its eastern setting. Owing to the dusty roads in Palestine, it was customary to provide for guests to have their sandles removed and their feet to be washed. This was a task done by a servant of low degree. No such provision had been made by the disciples as they gathered in the upper room for the last passover supper with Jesus. So after supper Jesus gave them an illustrated sermon by girding Himself with a towel and washing the disciples feet. Of course this was to teach them the great lesson of humility. Jesus took the lowliest place, and said, *"If I then, your Lord and Master, have washed your feet, ye also ought to wash one anothers feet."* But it is not to this lesson of humility we turn for guidance just now, but rather to the conversation between our Lord and Peter. When Jesus came to Peter, he said to the Lord, *"Thou shalt never wash my feet"*. We can quite understand his feelings, but Jesus said, *"If I wash thee not, thou hast no part with me"*. Then Peter went all the other way, saying, *"Not only my feet but my hands and my head also"*. Then Jesus replied, *"He that is washed* (bathed) *needeth not save to wash his feet, but is clean every whit."* There is a great spiritual lesson here for us. The word *'washed'* in this verse means washed all over - bathed. This refers to our conversion experience, to that precious cleansing; yet our feet may become dusty. We may err and fail our Lord, therefore we need daily washing. We must always come to Jesus for cleansing whenever we may be conscious that we have sinned or done wrong in any way. This is like having our feet washed, we should understand that there is this twofold aspect of our Lord's forgiving grace. We do not lose our salvation every time we sin, we do not lose relationship although we may lose fellowship because of sin. For that reason we need to constantly know the cleansing of the precious blood of Jesus. Peter's idea of being washed all over again was not necessary, but he did need this daily washing and so do we. I used to know a man who would often use this quaint phrase in his prayers, but I see what he meant: "Lord, help us keep short accounts with Thee".

Just a chorus today:-

Cleanse me from my sin Lord,
Put Thy power within, Lord;
Take me as I am, Lord,
And make me all Thine own.
Keep me day by day, Lord,
Underneath Thy sway, Lord;
Make my heart Thy palace,
And Thy royal throne.

Y.L.C. Chorus.

PRAYER

Almighty and everlasting God, who hatest nothing that Thou hast made, and dost forgive the sins of all them that are penitent: create and make in us new and contrite hearts. Amen.

Book of Common Prayer.

TWENTY-SECOND DAY

Read: John 14:1-11

Jesus said: *"Let not your heart be troubled: ye believe in God, believe also in me."* v.1.

"The three-fold cure for a troubled heart" is the title given to a greatly comforting sermon preached on the first three verses of John 14 by Dr. Herbert Lockyer, in the Baptist Church at Bromley, Kent, on his last Sunday in this country before flying over to the United States to be with his son, after the recent 'Home-call' of his dear wife. I have given much thought to what I should write for you today, and I have come to the conclusion that I cannot do better than just give you some gleanings from that blessed message our dear brother preached then. I have a tape-recording of that sermon and have just been listening to it again. For the sake of anyone who may not know Dr. Lockyer, let me say he is a very gifted preacher, and a prolific writer of books about the Bible. A tall, powerful man, at 92 years of age he still had a strong preaching voice. I was privileged to meet him when he preached in my church at Catford, some years ago. I will give you a short transcript from his tape-recorded sermon on John 14:1-4.

"Believe also in me." said Jesus. These men believed in God, *"believe also* (and I have put a circle round that word in my Bible) *in ME."*

"Jesus was going away and these men were sorely troubled. And there is always someone going away. Four Sundays ago, after 66 years of marriage, my dear wife of 92 years of age, died in my arms, left me for the Father's Home. Her precious dust lies buried in God's green acre, but she, herself, is with the Lord she loved. I can assure you Heaven is more real to my heart since her home-going, and I have found great consolation in these words we are considering this evening. So here we have a threefold cure for troubled hearts.

1. Faith in Christ. V.1. *'Believe also in me.'*

2. Faith in Heaven. V.2. *'I go to prepare a place.'*

3. Faith in His return. V.3. *'I will come again.'*."

Isn't that lovely!

I am waiting for the dawning
Of that bright and blessed day,
When the darksome night of sorrow
Shall have vanished far away;
When for ever with the Saviour,
Far beyond this vale of tears,
I shall swell the song of worship
Through the everlasting years.

I am waiting for the coming
Of the Lord who died for me;
Oh, His words have thrilled my spirit,
"I will come again for thee":
Faith can almost hear His footfall
On the threshold of the door,
And my heart, my heart is longing
To be with Him evermore.

Samuel T. Francis,
(1834-1925).

PRAYER

The Lord's Prayer.

Lord Jesus, what a meeting that will be! How I praise Thee for this word of Thine, "I will come again and receive you unto myself". This is my hope and stay.
Amen.

TWENTY-THIRD DAY

Read: John 15:17-26

"But when the Comforter is come, whom I will send unto you from the Father, even the Spirit of truth, which proceedeth from the Father, he shall testify of me."
v.26.

The first part of this chapter was our subject for one day in the previous book, so I have chosen three verses for today. Comforter - what a lovely noun! Comfort-er, that is someone who brings comfort. The Holy Spirit is called the Comforter in our Bibles, although the actual name, Paraclete, means, 'One who comes alongside to help'. A Strengthener. Let me give a simple illustration as I think it will help. You see that man pushing a barrow-load of goods up hill. He is finding it a bit much, every step he takes seems to be slower. Watch! I see another man who looks strong, and as he catches up he puts out his arm and gives a hand to help push. Immediately I notice the wheels of the barrow move quicker, and the poor fellow who found it such a struggle to continue now quickens his pace as the load seems so much lighter. Look again, they are over the brow of the hill now. What a difference it made to have the help of another, what a comfort! Now this is just what our Lord promised His followers. He would send *'another comforter'* John 14:16. I like the word *'another'* in that verse because it really means, 'another of the same kind'. Jesus who had been such a help to those disciples was soon to leave them, but He would not leave them *'orphans'* - helpless - He would send someone like Himself to be with them as their helper, their strengthener. And so the Holy Spirit has been called Jesus' other self. The blessed fact is that this same Holy Spirit is still with us, comforting, giving help up the hills of life. He shall be with you for ever, said Jesus. And, note, *"He shall testify of me."* To testify is to witness to, to affirm, to support. What we need to do is to rely upon the presence of the Holy Spirit dwelling in our hearts, as we do we find He gives us His grace and power. He is always coming alongside to help.

Joys are flowing like a river,
Since the Comforter has come;
He abides with us for ever,
Makes the trusting heart His home.

Blessed quietness, holy quietness,
What assurance in my soul!
On the stormy sea, He speaks peace to me,
How the billows cease to roll.

Bringing life, and health, and gladness,
All around this heavenly Guest;
Banished unbelief and sadness,
Changed our weariness to rest.

Like the rain that falls from heaven,
Like the sunlight from the sky,
So the Holy Ghost is given,
Coming on us from on high.

Mamie Payne Ferguson.

PRAYER

Almighty God, I thank Thee for the precious gift of Thy Holy Spirit. May I ever remember He is with me to strengthen and help me. Amen.

TWENTY-FOURTH DAY

Read: John 16:1-14

"When He the Spirit of truth is come, he shall guide you into all truth.....He shall glorify me."

v.13 & 14.

Now today, a little more unfolding of the Person and work of the Holy Spirit. You will notice I said, Person and work, because it would be quite wrong to think of the Holy Spirit merely as a force or power emanating from God. And the doctrine of the Personality of the Holy Spirit does not simply rest upon the fact that the personal pronoun 'He' is always used in the Gospels. We read of the *"Mind of the Spirit"*, *"The love of the Spirit"*, *"The Spirit knows"*, He *"Teaches"*, He is called, *"The eternal Spirit"*. We are told not to *"grieve the Spirit"*. All such words imply personality. You cannot grieve an 'it'. Electricity is a power, but it does not have 'mind'.

This third Person of the Holy Trinity is the Executive of the Godhead. Let me put it like this: GOD - The Father loved us; The Son died for us; The Holy Spirit makes real in our experience, the love of the Father and the work of the Son. Thus all three Persons in this Tri-une God are involved in our redemption. Of course there is a mystery about this doctrine of the Trinity: Three in One and One in Three, but this may help a little. From the sun we receive its yellow rays which give us light, the red rays which give heat, and the violet rays which bring health. Only one sun but its operations for our benefit are threefold. Light, warmth and life. All over the world wherever and whenever the sun shines on people it gives light, and heat and health. Only one sun but we have this threefold sense of its ministry. Often in church architecture you will see what is called a trefoil. This is a design in church windows or in its woodwork made by three circles each overlapping one another to form the shape of a three-leafed clover. It is an architectural way of symbolizing the Trinity. Three complete circles put together to form this shape, three in one, yet one in three. Of course no human illustration could be adequate to fully express so great a mystery, but we can, and should thank God for every work of grace made real in experience by the Holy Spirit of truth who guides us into all truth and who glorifies Christ.

Holy, Holy, Holy! Lord God Almighty!
Early in the morning our songs shall
rise to Thee:
Holy, Holy, Holy! merciful and mighty!
God in three Persons, Blessed Trinity!

Holy, Holy, Holy! Lord God Almighty!
All Thy works shall praise Thy name,
In earth, and sky, and sea:
Holy, Holy, Holy! merciful and mighty!
God in three Persons, Blessed Trinity!

Reginald Heber,
(1783-1826).

PRAYER

Almighty God, we worship Thee that Thou art for ever Holy. We thank Thee for the gracious gift of Thy Spirit who dwelling in our hearts is ever seeking to reveal Thy truth to us, and glorify Christ Jesus through us. Guard my heart that I may never grieve Thee. Amen.

TWENTY-FIFTH DAY

Read: John 17:1-11

"This is life eternal, that they might know Thee, the only true God, and Jesus Christ, whom Thou hast sent." v.3.

KNOWING GOD - that, said Jesus, is *"life eternal"*. Not knowing about God, as one would by the study of Theology; no, not intellectually knowing Him, but having a knowledge which is heart-felt and personal. The basis of such knowledge is personal relationship with God through Christ, and so our Lord, quite naturally, couples Himself with God in a way in which it would be impossible were Jesus not divine. Read v.3 again and you will see that is true. *"Believe also in me"*, said Jesus, John 14:1. It is true that to really know a person, one needs to live with him or her. You get to know God by living in the light of His Presence day by day. So it is that Paul writes about, *"increasing in the knowledge of God"*. Col. 1:10. Also, Peter says, *"Grow in grace and in the knowledge of our Lord and Saviour, Jesus Christ."* 2 Peter 3:18. *"The natural man receiveth not the things of the Spirit of God, for they are foolishness unto him: neither can he know them, because they are spiritually discerned* (understood)." 1 Cor. 2:14.

Living in the light of God, we are renewed in the spirit of our mind. Our thoughts and ways change, we *"set our mind - affections - on things above"*. We *"seek the kingdom of God and His righteousness"*. And *"this is life eternal"*. Our knowledge of God becomes experimental, which means: derived from practice rather than theory. I would say there are three main factors which will bring us into a fuller knowledge of God, as *"the only true God"*, v.3, these are:

1. Knowledge of God's Word.

2. The practise of prayer as communion with God.

3. A spiritual appreciation of the value of Christ in the service of Holy Communion - the receiving of His life with thanksgiving. Partaking of the bread and wine outwardly, while inwardly partaking of Christ who is our life.

I long to know Thee better day by day,
I want to draw much closer when I pray;
To listen more intently to Thy voice,
To let the things Thou choosest, be my choice.

I long to serve Thee better hour by hour,
Depending more entirely on Thy power;
I want to know much fully all Thy will,
To county upon each promise, and be still.

I long to keep more closely at Thy side,
To worship in Thy presence and abide;
I want to rest more calmly in Thy care,
Assured that Thou wilt keep me safely there.

I long to find new beauties in Thy Word,
To follow in the footsteps of my Lord;
And, oh, the greatest longing, through Thy grace,
Is that my eyes may see Thee Face to face.

Ada Habershon.

PRAYER

Oh, Lord, my God, I thank Thee that through divine grace Thou hast taught me my need of Thee, and that day by day I am getting to know Thee better. Lord, I just worship and adore Thee. Amen.

TWENTY-SIXTH DAY

Read: John 18:1-14

"When Jesus had spoken these words, he went forth with his disciples over the brook Cedron, where was a garden .....Jesus oft times resorted thither with his disciples."

v.1 & 2.

Of course the words Jesus spoke refers to His wonderful prayer recorded in chapter 17. Of all the sacred places on earth, surely the garden of Gethsemane ranks among the foremost. It was there that Jesus *'fought it out with the powers of darkness'* on that darkest of all nights in His earthly experience. John gives us the High Priestly prayer of the Lord, but it is the other three evangelists who tell of the Saviour's great conflict, and His prayer, *"Not my will but Thine be done"*. This garden was a place where they often went, and, no doubt, Jesus taught His disciples much as they sat in those quiet surroundings. Chronologically, the incidents given in Matthew 26:36-46 come just here between verses 2 and 3 of John 18. Jesus, having gone through the greatest battle of His life, apparently feeling a deep need for human companionship, yet being denied it because of the sleepiness of His friends, another blow now falls upon our Lord. Judas, who had professed to be one of His followers, came with soldiers and betrayed him with a kiss (although nothing is said here about the kiss of Judas) the other Gospels tell of that. Here John records the loving concern Jesus had for His own. Remember, it was dark and not all the soldiers would have seen the betrayal kiss. This no doubt explains verses 4-8. Jesus said to the soldiers, I am the one you are looking for, leave these others alone, let them go. Simon Peter was standing up for Jesus (v.10) but he did it in a wrong way! The Lord Jesus healed the man's ear, we read in Luke 22:51. Love must prove mightier than the sword! This was the last miracle in our Lord's healing ministry - and it was not on one of

His followers, but on one who had come to bind Him.

And can it be that I should gain
An interest in the Saviour's blood?
Died He for me, who caused His pain?
For me, who Him to death pursued?
Amazing love! how can it be
That Thou, my God, should'st die for me?

'Tis mystery all! The immortal dies!
Who can explore His strange design?
In vain the first born seraph tries
To sound the depth of love divine!
'Tis mercy all! let earth adore,
Let angel-minds inquire no more.

Long my imprisoned spirit lay,
Fast bound in sin and nature's night:
Thine eye diffused a quickening ray,
I woke, the dungeon flamed with light:
My chains fell off, my heart was free,
I rose, went forth, and followed Thee.

Charles Wesley,
(1707-1788).

PRAYER

Lord Jesus, I praise Thee that it was for sinners Thou didst die. It was upon one of Thine enemies Thou didst work Thy last healing miracle. Lord, I praise Thee that Thou art still working miracles of grace in human hearts. Thou dost set me free! Amen.

TWENTY-SEVENTH DAY

Read: John 19:1-22

"*And Pilate wrote a title, and put it on the cross.....*
JESUS OF NAZARETH KING OF THE JEWS." v.19.
Revelation 19:16. "*A name written, KING OF KINGS AND LORD OF LORDS.*"

What a full chapter we have today! One of the most action-packed chapters of the whole Gospel. Here we read about Jesus in His time of great suffering to redeem mankind. We may trace the record of Him being scourged, thus bearing our human suffering. We read of the crown of thorns - Jesus suffering the curse of sin for us; and of Him bearing His cross to a place called, Golgotha (Calvary) where He was crucified, and where He suffered the spiritual agony of being forsaken by God, bearing our sins in His body on the tree. On either side, was another who suffered for his own sin. Jesus suffered for the sins of others, He was in the midst - the central figure in all history. We even reckon time B.C. - Before Christ, or A.D. Ano Domini - In the year of our Lord!

Pilate could find no fault at all in Jesus. After His death, Joseph of Arimathea, a rich man and a secret disciple, begged the body of Jesus, and with the help of Nichodemus, laid it in his own hewn tomb in the garden, a quiet favourite place Jesus had known so well.

But among all these recorded incidents I would like us to think today about that inscription Pilate ordered to be displayed over His cross. It was a custom sometimes to write out what the person had been accused of, and Pilate wrote, THIS IS JESUS OF NAZARETH THE KING OF JEWS (compare all four Gospels and see the whole inscription as given above). Our Lord's accusers were offended at this and said to Pilate, "*write not KING OF THE JEWS, but that he said, I am king of the Jews*". "*What I have written, said Pilate, I have written.*" So that was an end to the argument. The declaration remained there in three languages for all to read. JESUS IS KING! That was the last testimony. It will be the first witness when He comes back again to take up His rightful place and reign, for we read in Revelation of Him upon a white horse and His name written, *"KING OF KINGS AND LORD OF LORDS."* See Rev. 19:9-16.

Jesus shall reign where'er the sun
Doth his successive journeys run;
His kingdom stretch from shore to shore,
Till moons shall wax and wane no more.

Peoples and realms of every tongue
Dwell on His love with sweetest song;
And infant voices shall proclaim
Their early blessings on His name.

Blessings abound where'er He reigns:
The prisoner leaps to lose his chains,
The weary find eternal rest,
And all the sons of want are blest.

Where He displays His healing power
Death and the curse are known no more;
In Him the tribes of Adam boast
More blessings than their father lost.

Issac Watts,
(1674-1748).

PRAYER

"Even so, Come, Lord Jesus". Amen.

The Lord's Prayer.

Gloria.

TWENTY-EIGHTH DAY

Read: John 20:1-18.

"Woman, why weepest thou?
Whom seekest thou?" v.15.
"Jesus saith unto her, Mary. She turned herself, and
saith unto Him, Rabboni!" v.16.

In Psalm 30:5 we read, *"Weeping may endure for a night, but joy cometh in the morning."* How true that was to Mary's experience on that resurrection morning! Mary was so sad, because they had taken her Lord, and with wicked hands had put Him to death. Then there was even more sadness when coming to the tomb she found that His precious body had gone. Can you imagine the turmoil in Mary's heart; what consternation, as yet another sad blow had fallen upon this devoted follower of Jesus. Then, breaking in upon the darkness of her soul, she sees two angels and they ask, *"Woman, why are you weeping?"* She replies, *"Because they have taken away my Lord, and I know not where they have laid him."* Mary said, *'they'*? Useful word that, when we don't know who! Poor bewildered Mary! Did she mean the soldiers? or the chief priests? or, or, ? Then without waiting further, she turned herself backward, and saw someone else. This stranger then asked her, *"Why are you weeping? Who are you seeking?"* Through her tears she manages to say, *"Sir, if you have taken him away,"* thinking him to be the gardener, *"tell me where you have laid him"*. Again Mary jumped to a wrong conclusion. Next what did she hear? Her name, *"Mary"*. She recognized His voice, and responded, *"Rabboni"*. The One she had been looking for was there all the time! And He was alive! As far as we know, *"MARY"* was the first word which came from the Risen Master, and it transformed everything for her. It was JESUS speaking in resurrection power, that always makes all the difference. It turned Mary's sorrow into joy, her perplexities into peace, her fearfulness into faithfulness, as she goes, in response to His word, and tells the disciples she had seen the Lord, and that He IS ALIVE. May we all know throughout this day, the Word of the Master coming to us in resurrection power. It is always a transforming experience!

Thou whose name is called Jesus,
Risen Lord of life and power,
Oh, it is so sweet to trust Thee,
Every day and every hour;
Of Thy wondrous grace I sing,
Saviour, Counsellor and King.

Thou canst keep my feet from falling,
Even my poor wayward feet:
Thou who dost present me faultless,
In Thy righteousness complete;
Jesus, Lord, in knowing Thee,
Oh, what strength and victory!

Oh, what joy to trust Thee, Jesus,
Mighty Victor o'er the grave,
And to learn amid earth's shadows
Thine unceasing power to save!
Only those who prove Thee know,
What the grace Thou dost bestow.

Jean Sophia Pigott.

PRAYER

Almighty Saviour, cause me to recognize Thy voice when Thou dost speak Thy Word in grace to my soul. And may I respond to thee. Amen.

TWENTY-NINTH DAY

Read: John 20:26-31

"Many other signs truly did Jesus.....which are not written in this book: but these are written that ye might believe that Jesus is the Christ, the Son of God, and that believing ye might have life through His name." v.30 & 31.

Here John gives his reason for writing, and these two last verses in chapter 20 could well bring this Gospel to a close. That is why some have considered chapter 21 was really written as a post-script - a kind of after-thought. It is a chapter that stands alone, but has a great message as we shall see. Those blessed words of Jesus spoken to Thomas which we read just now have been much appreciated by so many souls who, through the years, have been beset by doubts. Poor doubting Thomas, as we call him, yet God has been pleased to use his doubting experience to encourage others who have their doubts. How gracious Jesus was to this sincere believer who for a while had succumbed to doubts about the resurrection. It seems that Jesus went out of His way to help Thomas over the stile (v.27). It worked! With adoring wonder Thomas declares, *"My Lord, and my God."* Then we have that, for all time, comforting verse: *"Blessed are they that have not seen, and yet have believed."*

Well, John wants to draw his record of the life of Christ to a close on that note, so he says, there were of course many other things that Jesus did which he has not been able to record, *"But these are written that ye might believe that Jesus is the Christ, the Son of God; and that believing ye might have life through his name."* So, in summing up his Gospel John draws together the two key-words: LIFE and BELIEVE. The word '*LIFE*' occurs 22 times, and the word '*BELIEVE*' 30 times in this book.

You can, therefore, see how very important it is to

believe in the Lord Jesus Christ. As Paul says in Romans 10:9 & 10, *"If thou shalt confess with thy mouth the Lord Jesus, and shalt believe in thine heart that God hath raised him from the dead thou shalt be saved. For with the heart man believeth unto righteousness; and with the mouth confession is made unto salvation."*

Redemption! Oh, wonderful story -
Glad message for you and for me:
That Jesus has purchased our pardon,
And paid all the debt on the tree.

Believe it, O sinner, believe it;
Receive the glad message - 'tis true;
Trust now in the crucified Saviour,
Salvation He purchased for you.

No longer shall sin have dominion,
Thou present to tempt and annoy,
For Christ in His blessed redemption,
The power of sin shall destroy.

Accept now God's message of mercy;
To Jesus, oh, hasten today;
For He will receive him that cometh,
And never will turn him away.

S. M. Sayford.

PRAYER

The Lord's Prayer.

Now pray in your own words a prayer of faith in Jesus as God's Son, and your Saviour.

THIRTIETH DAY

Read: John 21:1-14

"Jesus said unto them, Bring of the fish which ye have caught. Simon Peter went up and drew the net to land full of great fish, an hundred and fifty and three."

v.10/11.

Marvellous! Especially as they had toiled all night and caught nothing! It seems to me there was a reason for that. You think of the circumstances in this story: Jesus had been crucified, all their hopes in Him as a great national leader had faded. Then, on two occasions Jesus had re-appeared but went out of their sight. What were they to make of it all? Peter decided it was time that he did something so he said, *"I go a fishing."* It almost seems the others were only waiting for a lead, and they said, *"We also go with thee."* This was a decision made out of mere common sense. Do you think perhaps they should have made it a matter of prayer first, as to what they ought to do? Anyway, that night they worked all through and at the dawn of day they had not caught a single fish. Still further depressed, they are returning with an empty boat when someone calls out to them, *"Lads, have you any fish?"* I can hear the disappointment in their voices, the way they shouted out that, *"NO."* Then the stranger says, *"Try again, cast the net on the right side, and you will find some."* They did what He said, and the result we have read - a large haul, big fish, so big they counted them: 153; you don't count smaller ones! *"It's the Lord"*, said John. What a difference the presence of Jesus makes, even to daily work. Then Jesus prepared a meal for those poor tired fishermen, and after they had breakfast, he turned to Peter and said, *"Lovest thou me more than these?"* Is Jesus speaking about the fish or about the other disciples? You think it through, most commentators consider He was referring to the other disciples but they tell us it is difficult to say as the sentence is a little ambiguous. Either way there is a lesson for us to learn. After all Peter did say, *"Through all men forsake Thee, I will not."* But you know the story so well; Peter after that denied Jesus three times. By now he had certainly lost all that arrogant self confidence. The best Peter could say was, *"Thou knowest....."* On the other hand there could well be a challenge here, Do you love me more than these fish you have caught - more than the material things in life? What is our reply?

Saviour! Thy dying love
Thou gavest me
Nor should I ought withold,
Dear Lord, from Thee;
In love my soul would bow,
My heart fulfil its vow,
Some offering bring Thee now,
Something for Thee.

Give me a faithful heart -
Likeness to Thee -
That each departing day
Henceforth may see
Some work of love begun,
Some deed of kindness done,
Some wanderer sought and won,
Something for Thee.

Rev. S. D. Phelps.

PRAYER

Pray for forgiveness. Wait upon God, and renew your strength.

SECTION TWELVE

FIRST DAY

Read: Psalm 119:1-8

"Blessed are the undefiled (blameless R.S.V.) in the way who walk in the law of the LORD. Blessed are they that keep his testimonies, and that seek Him with the whole heart." v.1 & 2.

Recently I received a letter from a friend who makes use of these Daily Readings, and in it she said: "How I have proved the Lord during these past weeks in so many ways. I had an attack of Angina and consequently had to rest quite a lot, so I caught up with my odd bits of needlework etc. Whilst doing so I was enabled to learn the 119th Psalm off by heart - all 176 verses, and what a blessing it has been to my soul!"

This series of Readings was originally produced as twelve duplicated books, the final one now becomes Section Twelve in this volume. I had been praying about the plan for this, the last book in this series, and it came to me that this Psalm could well be our subject, so for the next three weeks we will see what the Lord has to say to us all from this longest of all the 150 Psalms. This is a unique Psalm in many ways: Matthew Henry in his commentary says, "This is a Psalm by itself, like none of the rest; it excels them all."

Note first, this Psalm is divided into 22 equal parts, each having eight verses. In the A.V. Bible each section is headed by a letter from the Hebrew alphabet, Aleph, Beth, Gimel, Daleth, and so on. The reason for this is that in Hebrew every verse in each section begins with the same letter, A, B, etc. This is a most remarkable literary construction, although, of course, it is lost when translated. The R.S.V. omits the names of each letter heading these sections, but leaves a space between each one. Our thought for today is in the first two verses: *"BLESSED are the undefiled in the way - the upright, sincere, blameless.*" They walk in the law of JEHOVAH, they keep His testimonies, they seek Him with their whole heart!

That is the type of person God wants us to be, sincere, unblamable, wholehearted about our religion - our faith. Seek God with all your heart and you will find Him, and be blest by Him. See Jeremiah 29:11-13.

True-hearted, whole-hearted, faithful and loyal,
King of our lives, by Thy grace we will be!
Under Thy standard, exalted and royal,
Strong in Thy strength we will battle for Thee!

True-hearted, whole-hearted, fullest allegiance
Yielding henceforth to our glorious King!
Valiant endeavour and loving obedience
Freely and joyously now would we bring.

Frances Ridley Havergal,
(1836-1879).

PRAYER

"O Lord, forgive what I have been, sanctify what I am; and order what I shall be, through Jesus Christ my Lord. Amen."

The Lord's Prayer.

SECOND DAY

Read: Psalm 119:9-16

"Thy word have I hid in my heart that I might not sin against Thee." v.11.

It is related that the great American evangelist, D. L. Moody, when giving to one of his converts a Bible, wrote on the fly-leaf:

"This Book will keep you from sin; sin will keep you from this book!"

How true that is! No wonder David purposed that he would hide the Word of God in his heart. When I was a boy I learnt many verses of Scripture by heart. My brother and I had the privilege of being brought up in a Christian home, and our mother taught us numerous texts, also many hymns. We learnt them by memory just for the fun of memorizing, but mother knew the value of hiding God's Word in our hearts! Many passages of Scripture and verses of hymns still readily come to mind after all these years. Today's verse begins with *"THY WORD"*, and you would find it very interesting to go through this Psalm and underline those two words each time they occur. I did that in one of my Bibles, and can see at a glance what a prominent position they command in this Psalm.

Much of what David says refers to God's holy Word, he uses different words to describe his subject and you should make a note of these. Let me give you a list:

1.	God's law;	2.	His way;
3.	His testimonies;	4.	His commandments;
5.	His precepts;	6.	His word;
7.	His judgments;	8.	His righteousness;
9.	His statutes;	10.	His truth.

Now go over these eight verses and note: verse 9. An important question and his satisfactory answer; v.10.

His determination and prayer to be kept; v.11, reading God's Word with a spiritual purpose; v.12, *"Teach me"*; v.13. What God taught him, he passes on to others; v.14. Here is spiritual JOY; v.15. The blessed exercise of MEDITATION - serious, quiet thought; v.16. *"I will delight in, and not forget Thy law."* This illustrates what is meant by *"hiding God's Word in our hearts"*. The more you know the more you will grow. Build up yourself in your most holy faith. Jude 20 and 21.

The Spirit breathes upon the Word,
And brings the truth to sight;
Precepts and promises afford
A sanctifying light.

A glory gilds the sacred page,
Majestic, like the sun;
It gives a light to every age;
It gives, but borrows none.

Let everlasting thanks be Thine,
For such a bright display
As makes a world of darkness shine
With beams of heavenly day.

My soul rejoices to pursue
The steps of Him I love,
Till glory breaks upon my view,
In brighter worlds above.

William Cowper,
(1731-1800).

PRAYER

"O Lord, open Thou mine eyes, that I may behold wondrous things out of Thy law." Amen.

THIRD DAY

Read: Psalm 119:17-24

"Open Thou mine eyes, that I may behold wondrous things out of Thy law." v.18.

Here we have a prayer which we should pray every day. To some people the Bible is simply 'literature'. Many today think of it as being fables and folk-law. To the sincere believer who comes humbly to be taught by the Spirit of God, this is indeed The Word of God. Of course, the Psalmist would not have had the whole Bible as we know it, he probably had but little more than the writings of Moses. To him, here was the source of divine revelation, and he knew the 'comfort of the Scriptures', David also realised his need for the guidance of the Holy Spirit. That is why he prayed this prayer for illumination. Paul tells us: *"The natural man receiveth not the things of the Spirit of God: for they are foolishness unto him: neither can he know them because they are spiritually discerned."* 1 Cor. 2:14. In John 14:17 & 26 we find the Lord Jesus promised to send the Holy Spirit to be our teacher. *"He shall bring all things to your remembrance, whatsoever I have said unto you."* This surely was the main factor in the writing of the Gospels. The Holy Spirit who caused the Word to be written is the one upon whom we should rely as our teacher. He will interpret to believing hearts its inner meaning, and thus we will grow in grace as we grow in knowledge of God. We must be willing to be taught and to be guided by the Lord through what we read in His Word. There needs to be a blending of God's plan and our desire. 2 Timothy 2:15 is a verse of Scripture which was given me at my baptism, and again after I received the call of God to devote my life to the ministry of His Word. *"Study to show thyself approved unto God, a workman that needeth not to be ashamed, rightly dividing the word of truth."*

Open my eyes that I may see
Glimpses of truth Thou hast for me;
Place in my hands the wonderful key
That shall unclasp and set me free.

Silently now I wait for Thee,
Ready, my God, Thy will to see
Open my eyes, illumine me,
Spirit divine!

Open my mouth and let me bear
Tidings of mercy everywhere;
Open my heart and let me prepare
Love with Thy children thus to share.

Open my mind that I may read
More of Thy love in word and deed;
What shall I fear while yet Thou dost
lead?
Only for light from Thee I plead.

Clara H. Scott & Frederick P. Morris.

PRAYER

Blessed Lord, help me always to remember to seek Thy guidance as I read Thy Holy Word. Open my eyes to see its truths. Make the Book live to me, O Lord. Show me myself, and show me my Saviour, and make the Book live to me. Amen.

FOURTH DAY

Read: Psalm 119:25-32

"My soul cleaveth unto the dust: quicken thou me according to thy word." v.25.

I was giving a message to boys and girls in our church one Sunday, and to illustrate how easy it is to be drawn on to the downward path I had fixed up a sheet of thin white card on a frame. Behind this (unseen by the children) I held a powerful magnet, then as I offered up to the front of the card some oval nails it was possible for them to be drawn across from side to side and up and down as I moved the magnet about.

The Psalmist was aware of unseen, yet powerful, forces which caused his soul to be drawn down earthward. *"My soul cleaveth to the dust"*, he says, and prayed this prayer, *"Quicken thou me according to Thy word."* Do you sometimes feel dull and lifeless spiritually? Are there times when your soul seems to cling to the dust? Then pray this prayer, "Lord quicken me". Produce in me new life. Paul uses this phrase in Ephesians 2:1 *"And you hath he quickened, who were dead in trespasses and sins."* Do not overlook the fact that spiritual life comes to us through God's Word, *"according to thy word."* The Word of God promises this quickening. In 1 Peter 1:23 we read: *"Being born again, not of corruptible seed, but of incorruptible, by the word of God, which liveth and abideth for ever."* Mind and heart, motives and purposes are all affected by the Word of God, and so it is that David says to God, *"Teach me thy statutes."* v.26. *"Make me to understand thy precepts."* v.27. *"Strengthen me."* v.28. *"Remove me from the way of lies."* v.29. *"The result is clear for us to see."* v.30. *"I have chosen the way of thy truth." "I have stuck to thy testimonies." "I will run the way of thy commandments."* v.31 & 32.

My magnet and nails demonstrated to the children that there is an unseen power which can pull us down.

But there is also the power of God ever seeking to draw us upward. Ask that God's unseen power may quicken you afresh that you may ever walk in His ways, and obey His will.

Breathe on me, Breath of God,
Fill me with life anew,
That I may love what Thou dost love,
And do what Thou wouldst do.

Breathe on me, Breath of God,
Until my heart is pure,
Until with Thee I will one will,
To do and to endure.

Breathe on me, Breath of God,
Till I am wholly Thine,
Till all this earthly part of me
Glows with Thy fire divine.

Edwin Hatch,
(1835-1889).

PRAYER

Almighty God, I praise Thee for the refreshing which comes to me through the power of Thy precious Word. Yes, Lord, that is what I need, fresh strength to live closer to Thee each day. Lord, I thank Thee that Thou dost give me that just now. Amen.

FIFTH DAY

Read: Psalm 119:33-40

"Give me understanding, and I shall keep thy law; yea, I shall observe it with my whole heart." v.34.

"My whole heart", we have seen that important little phrase before: v.2 & 10. It is tragic if a Christian is half-hearted in worship and witness to Christ. God calls for whole-hearted allegiance to Himself and His truth. Whole-heartedness may be demonstrated by the way we use our time, our talents, and our money in the service of the Lord. It was the late Dr. F. B. Meyer who once said that at one time he handed over the keys to all the rooms in his heart except one, that key he kept back for himself. But the Lord dealt with him about that one key, and at last he made a full surrender and handed over the key of that room to God. When Dr. Meyer did that the Lord came into his life in a greater way than ever before and God used His servant to bring salvation and sanctification to many other lives. *"Blessed are they that seek him with the whole heart." "With my whole heart have I sought thee, O let me not wander from thy commandments."*

Seeking God, and serving God with the whole heart can be summed up in the one word 'SINCERITY'. A sincere Christian is a whole-hearted Christian. There is a lovely hymn in the N.Y.L.C. hymn book; it begins: "Thou didst give Thyself for me......" When I first heard it sung by a choir in one of their big meetings, it made a great impression on me. The words of the chorus can illustrate what we are thinking about just now, so I will give it.

All my days, and all my hours:
All my will, and all my powers;
All the pasion of my soul,
Not a fragment - but the whole
Shall be Thine, dear Lord,
Shall be Thine, dear Lord.

When God said to Abram, *"I am the Almighty God, walk before me, and be thou perfect."* (Gen. 17:1). He meant this perfection of sincerity. If we are going to *'walk before God'* we must be 'sincere'.

Have you given God all the keys yet?

Take my life, and let it be
Consecrated, Lord, to Thee;
Take my moments and my days,
Let them flow in ceaseless praise.

Take my hands and let them move
At the impulse of Thy love;
Take my feet and let them be
Swift and beautiful for Thee.

Take my will, and make it Thine;
It shall be no longer mine.
Take my heart; it is Thine own;
It shall be Thy royal throne.

Take my love; my Lord, I pour
At Thy feet its treasure store,
Take myself, and I will be
Ever, only, ALL for Thee.

Frances Ridley Havergal,
(1836-1879).

PRAYER

The Lord's Prayer.

Use this hymn as your own personal prayer of consecration.

SIXTH DAY

Read: Psalm 119:41-48

"*I will walk at liberty: for I seek thy precepts* (A rule of action, guide to moral conduct)."

v.45.

Have you seen that arresting little phrase: "Love God, and do as you like."? I wonder what may be your first reaction as you see those words? It might well be, 'If I love God, I cannot do as I like.' Think again! "Love toward God" is the governing phrase in this sentence. If we truly love God we will only wish to do what He wishes. So His will becomes our will, His likes are our likes. We can do as we like because our desires are being governed by this principle of loving God. This verse in the R.S.V. is: *"I shall walk at liberty, for I have sought thy precepts."* Here is true liberty! A worldly person thinks that the commands of God produce bondage, in fact God's commandments are given to release us from our bondage to sin. Let me illustrate: You may be walking down a road and you see a sign, "DANGER KEEP OUT". A foolish person could say, "Why should I? I am not having my liberty restricted by a notice like that! I will go where I please." A sensible person will read the notice, and know there must be a good reason for it being there, so he keeps out. By obeying the commandment, KEEP OUT, he is kept from some danger. He is the truly free person; the other one may use his so-called liberty and find himself actually in bondage - especially should some masonry fall on his head!

Take for instance, the simple notice we sometimes see in a park: "KEEP OFF THE GRASS". Why is that put there? Because if everyone walked over it, before long all that beautiful lush grass would be gone, spoiled under many feet. Yes, there is quite a lot of sense in the ordinary prohibitions in life. It's always best to obey them! So with the commands of God. *"I will walk at liberty."* HOW? I seek THY PRECEPTS.

I am Thine, O Lord; I have heard Thy voice,
And it told Thy love to me;
But I long to rise in the arms of faith,
And be closer drawn to Thee.

Draw me nearer.....nearer blessed Lord,
To the cross where Thou hast died;
Draw me nearer, nearer, nearer blessed Lord
To Thy precious wounded side.

Oh, the pure delight of a single hour
That before Thy throne I spend,
When I kneel in prayer, and with Thee, my God,
I commune as friend with Friend.

Fanny J. Crosby.

PRAYER

O Lord, fill us, we beseech Thee, with adoring gratitude to Thee for all Thou art for us, to us, and in us; fill us with love, joy, peace, and all the fruits of the Spirit. Amen.

(Christina Rossetti).

SEVENTH DAY

Read: Psalm 119:49-56

"This is my comfort in my affliction: for thy word hath quickened me." v.50.

Primarily, affliction means distress of mind. It may be brought about by grief, trouble, sorrow, or sickness. The word takes in more than physical illness, although that is one form of affliction; but a healthy person may be afflicted. It seems the kind of distress David was thinking about was the direct result of hurtful, nasty things said about him by people. *"The proud have had me greatly in derision."* v.51. Whatever such folk might say, he determined to continue to live well pleasing to God, and he comforted himself by remembering God's judgments of old. (v.52). To deride means to ridicule, to laugh at with scorn, to mock, to belittle; and no one likes that! Such derision David called his affliction, but the jeers of men only drove him into the arms of God and there he found comfort.

Oh, how often the Lord's persecuted saints have found comfort in God's Word! There may be times when we are so mentally distressed, so afflicted by all kinds of opposition and trouble that we scarcely know what to do. Do you remember what the apostle James says about being afflicted? *"Is any afflicted, let him PRAY."* James 5:13. When you may be smarting under the scorn and derision of the ungodly, pray. Pray guided by the Scriptures, and you will know in a much fuller way than ever before the value of the friendship of the Lord Jesus. David's comfort came, he tells us, through a quickening of his spirit as he turned once again to God's Word. Read Isaiah 53: especially verses 3 and 4 and see how the Lord was afflicted. Notice too what He did when afflicted - v.7. As we turn from our afflictions to God's eternal love, we are quickened by His resurrection life being made manifest in us again and again.

What a Friend we have in Jesus,
All our sins and griefs to bear;
What a privilege to carry
Everything to God in prayer.
Oh, what peace we often forfeit,
Oh, what needless pain we bear;
All because we do not carry
Everything to God in prayer.

Have we trials and temptations?
Is there trouble anywhere?
We should never be discouraged;
Take it to the Lord in prayer.
Can we find a friend so faithful
Who will all our sorrows share?
Jesus knows our every weakness;
Take it to the Lord in prayer.

Joseph Scriven,
(1820-1886).

PRAYER

The Lord's Prayer.

Whatever is troubling you just now, tell God everything. Pour out all your distress, all your personal sorrow, into the Love-heart of God. Pour it all out as if pouring water out of a jug. Pour it out until the last drop has gone - like Hannah did in 1 Samuel 1:10-18. Then come away refreshed - quickened.

"Bless the Lord, O my soul."

EIGHTH DAY

Read: Psalm 119:57-64

"I thought on my ways, and turned my feet unto thy testimonies." v.59.

Isn't this just what we all have to do at times? It is good for us to think on our ways, and notice if we are adhering to the truth of God's Word. It is so easy for us to deviate unless we are constantly watchful. We have a subtle foe! Little wonder that the apostle Peter exhorts: *"Be sober, be vigilant; because your adversary the devil, as a roaring lion, walketh about, seeking whom he may devour. Whom resist stedfast in the faith."* 1 Peter 5:8-9. First the Psalmist thought - thought before he acted - *"I thought on my ways"*; he had a spiritual check up on himself, and having realised his feet were not continuing in the right direction, he by a deliberate act of will *"turned his feet into the right way - into Thy testimonies"*. This Word of God is our instruction book; it is a map to show us the right way to go. It is very wonderful how the Holy Spirit teaches us, when we are willing, so that as we read He applies the inner teaching of the Word to our hearts. *"All Scripture is given by the inspiration of God, and is profitable for doctrine, for reproof, for correction, for instruction in righteousness: that the man of God may be perfect, throughly furnished unto all good works."* 2 Timothy 3:16-17. Note the FOUR things God's Word is said to do; and the purpose in verse 17. Like David, we must co-operate with the Spirit's guidance, we must think, and turn our feet into His ways. *"I made haste and delayed not to keep thy commandments."* v.60. How wise! Delay can lead to disaster. Once we know God's will, we must do it, looking to God for His strength and enabling grace.

Lord, Thy Word abideth,
And our footsteps guideth;
Who its truth believeth,
Light and joy receiveth.

When our foes are near us,
Then Thy Word doth cheer us,
Word of consolation,
Message of salvation.

When the storms are o'er us,
And dark clouds before us,
Then its light directeth,
And our way protecteth.

Who can tell the pleasure,
Who recount the treasure,
By Thy Word imparted
To the simple hearted.

Oh, that we discerning
Its most holy learning,
Lord, may love and fear Thee,
Evermore be near Thee.

Henry Williams Baker,
(1821-1877).

PRAYER

Almighty God, by Thy Spirit, help me to consider my ways. Teach me Thy way, O Lord, lead me, and strengthen me that I may ever be willing to turn my feet into the ways of Thy truth, through Jesus Christ my Lord. Amen.

NINTH DAY

Read: Psalm 119:65-72

"Before I was afflicted I went astray: but now have I kept Thy word." "It is good for me that I have been afflicted; that I might learn Thy statutes."

v.67 & v.71.

It is a wonderful blessing when as Christian believers we can see that God has a purpose in all He allows; when we realise that even our afflictions can turn out for our good. God is able to take hold of those things in life which we might consider as frustrations and trials, and so transform our attitude towards them that instead of them doing us harm they are the very things that can do us good. If you have asked God to keep you in His will and on the right path, don't be surprised when you find your way hedged in to keep you from going astray! The Psalmist came to see that before he was afflicted he went astray, but now - with the aid of those afflictions - he has kept God's Word. Therefore, seeing the great purpose God had for him, he could *"kiss the rod that chastened"*.

You know, human nature being what it is, we can so easily fail in our quest for God's best unless through the disciplines of life we come to see how frail we really are. No wonder David prayed, *"Make me to know how frail I am."* Psalm 39:4. Our trouble so often is that we just do not know how frail we are! God will use affliction to produce strength of character which would not otherwise be ours. He often does this through what we call ordinary circumstances of life. Among my collection of 'Verses & Quotes' I have one entitled, 'ENVIRONMENT': "Our environment is often but the answer to our prayers. We pray for patience and our Father sends us those who tax us to the utmost, for "tribulation worketh patience". We pray, "Lord increase our faith" and some hitherto unknown trial comes which calls for an increase of faith along a line we have not needed to exercise much faith before. We pray the love-chapter, and there comes across our path those who are selfish, jealous, arrogant and distasteful, where all natural love fails and only divine love will prevail." We have to learn the words in Romans 8:28 by HEART in more ways than one! Does this explain what has hitherto been inexplicable in your life? PRAY THIS HYMN.

In heavenly love abiding,
No change my heart shall fear;
And safe is such confiding,
For nothing changes here;
The storms may roar without me,
My heart may low be laid;
But God is round about me,
And can I be dismayed?

Wherever He may guide me,
No want shall turn me back;
My Shepherd is beside me,
And nothing shall I lack:
His wisdom ever waketh,
His sight is never dim;
He knows the way He taketh,
And I will walk with Him.

Anna L. Waring,
(1820-1910).

TENTH DAY

Read: Psalm 119:73-80

"I know, O Lord, that Thy judgments are right, and that Thou in faithfulness hast afflicted me." "Let, I pray Thee, thy merciful kindness be for my comfort."

v.75 & 76.

Yes, praise God, even amid all our afflictions and adversities God's merciful kindness will be our comfort. Let me share with you a verse which has been a blessing to me, and I am sure to many who have seen it. No, it is not a verse of Scripture although there is a whole lot of truth in it. But first, I will tell you how I came to have this verse. One of the happy experiences of my life and work has been that through the years many friends have kept in touch with us after they have moved elsewhere. During the war years two of our young ladies met Christian young men who were in this country attached to the Canadian Air Force. I had the pleasure of conducting both weddings for these young people, and soon after they left us to make their homes in Ontario. We have corresponded through the many years since and it has been a joy to receive news of them and their families, now grown up and to know of their activities in the Lord's work in Canada. A couple of years ago we received from one of these friends, a linen calendar on which this verse is printed: "God grant me the SERENITY to accept the things I cannot change; COURAGE to change the things I can: and WISDOM to know the difference." I have kept that, its worth thinking about! I have a feeling as you think over these words you will enter more fully into the experience of today's section of this Psalm, and the merciful kindness of God who grants SERENITY, COURAGE, and WISDOM.

O, safe to the Rock that is higher than I,
My soul in its conflicts and sorrows would fly;
So sinful, so weary, Thine, Thine would I be;
Thou blest "Rock of Ages" I'm hiding in Thee.

Hiding in Thee, hiding in Thee,
Thou blest "Rock of Ages"
I'm hiding in Thee.

How oft in the conflict, when pressed by the foe,
I have fled to my Refuge and breathed out my woe;
How often when trials like sea-billows roll,
Have I hidden in Thee, O Thou Rock of my soul.

W. O. Cushing.

PRAYER

The Lord's Prayer.

"Grant, we beseech Thee, merciful Lord, to Thy faithful people pardon and peace, that they may be cleansed from all their sins, and serve Thee with a quiet mind; through Jesus Christ our Lord. Amen."
(A fifth century prayer.)

ELEVENTH DAY

Read: Psalm 119:81-88

"Mine eyes fail for thy word, saying, When wilt thou comfort me? For I am become like a bottle in the smoke, yet do I not forget thy statutes." v.82/83.

"I am become like a bottle in the smoke." Whatever does he mean? Well, first, don't think of a glass bottle with which we are so familiar. Their bottles were made from skins of animals. The R.S.V. gives: *"I have become like a wine-skin in the smoke."* The reference here is to an old disused wine-skin bottle, hung up maybe for years in a smoky atmosphere. The leather would become all shrivelled up and wrinkled, no longer a thing of beauty or usefulness. This is how David felt at that time, the years were passing quickly, and with all sorts of troubles and afflictions, and the torments of his persecutors, he was feeling 'a bit worse for wear' as we say. What an apt illustration! As a youth he is described as *"ruddy* (rosy cheeks) *and of a beautiful countenance, and goodly to look to."* (1 Sam. 16:12). Now he feels his soul is faint, his health is failing, yet he is still hoping in God's Word. Something like the experience described by Paul in 2 Cor. 4:16, *"For which cause we faint not; but though our outward man perish, yet the inward man is renewed day by day."*

Do you feel a bit shrivelled up, like a wine-skin in the smoke, because of all you have been through lately? Then here is just the right word for you! Be sure you too can say, *"Yet I do not forget thy statutes."* Statutes - the written laws of God. *"Thou shalt love the Lord thy God with all thy soul and with all thy mind. This is the first and great commandment; and the second is like unto it, Thou shalt love thy neighbour as thyself; on these two commandments hang all the law and the prophets." "Lord have mercy upon us and incline our hearts to keep Thy law."* Amen. Now read: 2 Corinthians 4:16-18 and note the last two verses, they will be a blessing to you today!

All the way my Saviour leads me;
What have I to ask beside?
Can I doubt His tender mercy,
Who through life has been my Guide?
Heavenly peace, divinest comfort,
Here by faith in Him to dwell!
For I know what'er befalls me,
Jesus doeth all things well.
(repeat last two lines)

All the way my Saviour leads me,
Cheers each winding path I tread,
Gives me grace for every trial,
Feeds me with the Living Bread.
Though my weary steps may falter,
And my soul athirst may be,
Gushing from the Rock before me,
Lo! a spring of joy I see.

Fanny J. Crosby,
(1820-1915).

PRAYER

Blessed Lord, my God, Thou knowest how I have been feeling lately. I now turn my eyes away from my troubles and look afresh to Thee, for Thou wilt never leave me nor forsake me. Lord, how grateful I am to Thee for Thy Word which liveth and abideth for ever. Thou dost feed me with the Bread of heaven, I thank Thee. Amen.

TWELFTH DAY

Read: Psalm 119:89-96

"Unless thy law had been my delights, I should then have perished in mine affliction." v.92.

Ah! here is the secret of David's victory in his time of adversity. Looking over his experiences he sees what peril he had been in. He tells us that there was an awful possibility of his having perished in his affliction. What gave him the victory? To what does he ascribe the source of his strength and comfort? To the Word of God, which had all along been his delight. In fact here he sums up his experience by declaring, *"Unless thy law had been my delights, I should then have perished in my affliction."* Oh, there must be thousands since this Psalm was written who could agree with these words! Thousands, who amid the troubles of an earthly life, have found heavenly comfort in the law of the Lord. Turn back just one hundred Psalms, and you will read: *"The law of the LORD is perfect, converting the soul: the testimony of the LORD is sure, making wise the simple. The statutes of the LORD are right, rejoicing the heart: the commandment of the LORD is pure, enlightening the eyes."* (19:7-8). Read again the words underlined and you will see what God's Word does for you. Then note, David not only read the Word, he tells us it had been his *'delights'*. He appreciated the purpose for which it had been given; he understood the reason, and accepted the correction. But for that he feels he certainly would have perished in his afflictions. In the Epistle of Jude (v.20/21) we read: *"But ye, beloved, building yourselves up on your most holy faith, praying in the Holy Ghost, keep yourselves in the love of God, looking for the mercy of our Lord Jesus Christ unto eternal life."* God's Word becomes a delight to us when we gladly listen to what He has to say through it, and put that into daily practise in our lives. Thus are we KEPT BY THE POWER OF GOD.

How firm a foundation, ye saints of the Lord,
Is laid for your faith in His excellent Word!
What more can He say than to you He hath
said,
You who unto Jesus for refuge have fled?

Fear not, I am with thee, O be not dismayed!
I, I am thy God and will still give thee aid:
I'll strengthen thee, help thee, and cause
thee to stand,
Upheld by my righteous, omnipotent hand.

When through the deep waters I call thee to
go,
The rivers of grief shall not thee overflow:
For I will be with thee in trouble to bless:
And sanctify to thee thy deepest distress.

Richard Keen.

PRAYER

O God, who makest all things work together for good to those who love Thee, pour into my heart Thy steadfast love that I may ever delight in Thy truth.

Amen.

THIRTEENTH DAY

Read: Psalm 119:97-104

"O how I love thy law! It is my meditation all the day." "How sweet are thy words to my taste! Yea, sweeter than honey to my mouth!"

v.97 & 103.

As we read through this Psalm it is very evident that God's Word meant much to the writer. He had learned so much, he had been saved from so much wrong-doing. The Word of the LORD had often brought him much comfort, David had grown to love the laws of God. *"O how I love thy law!"*, he exclaims. Then maybe, remembering his childhood days he declares, *"How sweet are thy words to my taste, yea, sweeter than honey to my mouth."* I say, remembering his childhood days, because this illustration about honey may well refer to a custom they had in the East of encouraging little children to learn by putting a little honey on their writing tablets with the words they were to commit to memory. A lick of the honey helped no end! The words literally became sweet to their taste. It was a delight to learn, and, of course, it is always so much easier when we take pleasure in learning. Note how he learnt: *"It is my meditation all the day"*.

When God gave instruction to Joshua, He said, *"This book of the law shall not depart out of thy mouth; but thou shalt meditate therein day and night, that thou mayest observe to do according to all that is written therein: for then thou shalt make thy way prosperous, and then thou shalt have good success."* (Joshua 1:8). To meditate means to think deeply upon. A good plan is to take a verse, or thought from Scripture (perhaps something from these daily readings) and fix your mind on it for a few quiet moments before you start the day's activities, then whenever you have a few minutes let that thought recur in your mind. Read Joshua 1:8 again now, go over it thoroughly. Notice the words I have underlined - thought must develop into action. Then mark the conditional promise. Meditation can be very rewarding!

O Jesus Christ, grow Thou in me,
And all things else recede;
My heart be daily nearer Thee,
From sin be daily freed.

Each day let Thy supporting might
My weakness still embrace;
My darkness vanish in Thy light,
Thy life my death efface.

In Thy bright beams which on me fall,
Fade every evil thought;
That I am nothing, Thou art all,
I would be daily taught.

Make this poor self grow less and less,
Be Thou my life and aim;
Oh, make me daily through Thy grace
More meet to bear Thy name.

Johann Caspar Lavater,
(1741-1801).

PRAYER

The Lord's Prayer.

Blessed Lord, teach me so to 'read, mark, learn, and inwardly digest' Thy Word, that its truths shall grip my heart, and transform my life. I praise Thee for this means of grace. Amen.

FOURTEENTH DAY

Read: Psalm 119:105-112

"Thy word is a lamp to my feet, and a light to my path." v.105.

This was one of the verses of Scripture I learned by heart before I was ten years old. Its truth I have been learning ever since! What simple illustrations we find in this Psalm, and yet they are full of sublime truth. - *"A lamp to my feet"*, fulfilling my immediate need as I go through life one step at a time. A light to my path, showing the way ahead. I have often found the Lord speaking to my heart through some passage of His Word as I have read it day by day. The Holy Spirit will light up some verse, or passage, which contains sometimes, rebuke, or instruction, or solace: just as it is needed. Life depends on light for growth. Sight also depends upon light. And it has well been said, "The stops, as well as the steps, of a good man are ordered by the Lord." Sometimes what we read shows us a green light, and we move forward in the will of the Lord. At other times we see clearly a red light, and stop we must or go on at our peril! There are times when the light of God's Word shows amber - proceed but with caution, or apply the brakes and stop!

It is truly amazing how that all over the world, people of different cultures and languages have come into similar spiritual experiences of blessing simply through observing the teachings of the Bible. Light and life and liberty have come to men and nations through this lamp. I have just been reading an article in the current issue of The Word in Action, the British and Foreign Bible Society newspaper. This will interest you: "You can now read complete books of the Bible in 1,660 different languages. The entire Bible in 268 different languages, the complete New Testament in 453 languages, and individual books - like the Gospels and Psalms - have been translated into a further 939 different tongues." Praise God, wherever the Book goes, light goes. *"THY WORD IS A LAMP UNTO MY FEET, AND A LIGHT TO MY PATH."* Make use of the lamp!

We thank Thee, Lord, indeed,
That Thou Thy Word hast given,
To light our path in this dark world,
And safely guide to heaven.

To warn of sinful steps,
And point our road each day,
To keep us in the one safe path,
The straight and narrow way.

Bless those who with us read
Thy wondrous book of light,
That all of us with one desire
May strive to do the right.

As Thy commands we seek
Within Thy Word each day,
Teach us what Thou wilt have us do,
Then teach us to obey.

R. Hudson Pope.

PRAYER

The Lord's Prayer.

Heavenly Father, write Thy Word upon my heart and by Thy grace give me strength to obey. Keep me in the centre of Thy will. Amen.

FIFTEENTH DAY

Read: Psalm 119:113-120

"Thou art my hiding place and my shield; I hope in Thy Word." v.114.

There were times when David hid from Saul's jealousy in caves and dens, but he was always committing himself to the mercies of Jehovah that he could say in all truthfulness: *"THOU art my hiding place."* Deliverance from enemies may come sometimes by hiding away from them, yet at other times by using the shield of faith on the battlefield. Often the saints of every age have found God to be a hiding place in their times of distress. Satan may seek, in all kinds of ways, to oppose the children of God, but in HIM we are safe and secure. It was while David was sheltering in the cave of Adullam that he drew to himself a band of faithful men who afterwards protected him. In 2 Sam. 23:14 we read: *Saul sought David every day, but the LORD did not deliver him into his hand."* God's arm of protection was with His servant and so he could declare, *"Thou art my hiding place, and my shield."* It was not the caves and the woods that gave David shelter from his enemy, behind all was the providence of God. So it is with us, God may use all sorts of means to protect those who trust in Him, but behind them all is His divine providence and sovereign purposes. *"A hiding place"*, yes, and *"A shield"* - so our LORD takes care of us amid all the onslaughts of our enemy the devil. We can hide in Him, be shielded from every evil thing; kept by the power of God in the hour of temptation. So, says David, *"I hope in Thy word."* The Word of God becomes our shield when we accept and believe its message. The apostle Paul writes about *"the shield of faith"* in Ephesians 6:16. Two kinds of shields were used in battle, one was small and the other quite large to cover the whole body. It is this big shield that Paul uses to illustrate his message. This is brought out in the

Amplified Bible which reads, "*Lift up over all the* (covering) *shield of saving faith, upon which you can quench all the flaming missiles of the wicked* (one)."

My hope is built on nothing less
Than Jesus' blood and righteousness;
I dare not trust the sweetest frame
But wholly lean on Jesus' Name.
On Christ, the solid Rock I stand;
All other ground is sinking sand.

When darkness seems to veil His face
I rest on His unchanging grace;
In every high and stormy gale
My anchor holds within the veil.
On Christ the solid Rock I stand;
All other ground is sinking sand.

His oath, His covenant, and blood
Support me in the 'whelming flood
When all around my soul gives way,
He then is all my hope and stay.
On Christ, the solid Rock I stand;
All other ground is sinking sand.

Edward Mote,
(1797-1874).

PRAYER

Almighty God, I thank Thee that Thou art my shield and my hope is in Thee, and in Thy Word. Keep me near to Thee, protected by the shield of faith.

Amen.

SIXTEENTH DAY

Read: Psalm 119:121-128

"It is time for thee, LORD, to work: for they have made void thy law. Therefore I love thy commandments above gold; yea, above fine gold." v.126/127.

The world in which we live is very much the same in its attitude to the Word of God, as it was when David prayed this prayer: *"It is time for thee, LORD, to work: for they have made void Thy law."* Oh, how sad it is to see the general trend of things nowadays. How blind to God's truth are so many, indeed it is, as Paul wrote in 2 Cor. 4:4, *"The god of this world hath blinded the minds of them that believe not, lest the light of the glorious gospel of Christ, who is the image of God, should shine unto them."* Even science and technology are so often used by the god of this world, Satan. It is often, not that a thing is basically wrong, but the purpose for which it is used may be good or it can be evil. Take for instance, radio and television: there are many people who have come to know Christ through hearing the gospel by these means. In some remote parts of the world where no missionary has gone, people have heard the gospel through the wonderful work done by Trans-world radio, and other such broadcasting associations. Billy Graham and other Evangelists have reached untold millions of people through T.V. and souls have responded to the Saviour's love. For this we can indeed praise the Lord. But, oh, the immeasurable harm that has been perpetrated by evil men making use of these methods of communication! The prince of the power of the air has not been slow in making void - of none effect - the law of God by reaching the minds of men through radio and television. Note how helpless David felt as he cried, *"It is time for Thee to work"*. He realized if men's hearts were to be changed it must be God who does it. *"Therefore"*, said he, *"I love thy commandments above gold, yea above fine gold"*. Twentieth century believers need to be careful lest we be caught up in the trap of T.V. and Radio programmes which *"Make void God's law"*. If we love His commandments as David did we will know instinctively when to switch off!

Stand up for Jesus, Christian, stand!
Firm as a rock on ocean's strand!
Beat back the waves of sin that roll
Like raging floods around thy soul!

Stand up for Jesus, Christian, stand!
Send forth His Name o'er sea and land!
Spread ye His glorious Word abroad,
Till all the world shall own Him Lord!

Stand up for Jesus, Christian, stand!
Soon with the blest immortal band
We'll dwell for aye, life's journey o'er,
In realms of light on heaven's bright
shore.

George Duffield,
(1818-1888).

PRAYER

O Lord, it is time for Thee to work; make me a channel of Thy grace. Help me to stand up for Thy truth among those who seek to make void Thy law.
Amen.

SEVENTEENTH DAY

Read: Psalm 119:129-136

"The entrance of thy words giveth light; it giveth understanding to the simple." v.130.

What would you consider to be the most important word in this well known verse? As I was thinking about it myself, it appeared to me that the most important word here is surely the word, *"ENTRANCE"*. It is the entrance of God's Word that gives light to our souls. The light is there shining all the time, but it may be possible for the sun to be shining in the sky and for a room to still be dark just because we have not drawn aside the curtains! Do that, and sunshine fills the room. God is light and in HIM is no darkness at all, says John. Jesus said, *"I am the light of the world, he that followeth me shall not walk in darkness but shall have the light of life."* But we must *'follow'* Him! Of course we are using this word, *'light'* as a synonym. Often spiritual truths can be better understood by the use of 'picture language'. Two important words in this verse are the words, *'light'* and *'understanding'*. God's Word gives understanding to the simple - that means those who are humble enough to receive it. If a person comes to God's Word with a closed mind, that one will never receive the light and truth it teaches. It is the <u>entrance</u> of that Word which brings us spiritual illumination. It may often be just as we read in Isaiah 28:10, *"Precept upon precept, line upon line, here a little, and there a little."* Often there is a gradual unfolding of divine truth. Always keep your mind and heart open to God, that He may lead you on in the knowledge of Himself. My first introduction to Bible study was while I was in my 'teens, when a friend invited me to his home to study the Scriptures together one evening each week. Then I took up a correspondence course of systematic Bible study. Things I learned those days have never been lost. God has always more light to shine forth from His Word.

Receive, and you can then receive more! It is the "*entrance*" of the light which brings understanding!

Father of mercies, in Thy Word
What endless glory shines!
Forever be Thy Name adored
For these celestial lines.

Here the Redeemer's welcome voice
Spreads heavenly peace around;
And life and everlasting joys
Attend the blissful sound.

O may these hallowed pages be
My ever dear delight!
And still new beauties may I see,
And still increasing light.

Divine Instructor, gracious Lord,
Be Thou for ever near;
Teach me to love Thy sacred Word,
And view my Saviour there.

Anne Steele,
(1716-1778).

PRAYER

The Lord's Prayer.

Heavenly Father, by Thy Spirit guide me into the truths of Thy Holy Word that I may learn of Thee. Amen.

EIGHTEENTH DAY

Read: Psalm 119:137-144

"Thy word is very pure, therefore thy servant loveth it." "Thy righteousness is an everlasting righteousness, and thy law is the truth."
v.140 & 142.

Purity and truth go hand in hand. Here the Psalmist gives another reason for his obvious affection for the Word of God - it is very pure. Indeed to him it was like the pure gold from which the lampstand in the Tabernacle was made. God gave Moses instructions that a beautiful lampstand should be made of solid gold, beaten out of one piece. It had seven lamps each formed in the shape of an almond. There was a centre stem with one lamp at the top, and out from either side were three branches with more lamps. These lamps were filled with oil and gave light to the priests when they were serving the LORD in the Holy place. All of pure gold, and God's Word is pure, very pure; that was why David loved it!

It is most remarkable that where God's Word is received by people in any part of the world it has the same purifying affect on their lives. Its great declaration is, as we have it in v.142, *"Thy righteousness is an everlasting righteousness, and thy law is the truth."* The apostle Peter says of this pure Word of God, *"It liveth and abideth for ever"*. We are 'born again' by the Word of God which is incorruptible seed. See 1 Peter 2:22-23. And, says Peter, *"Ye have purified your souls in obeying the truth."* Paul also speaks of this purifying affect that the Word of God has upon our lives, *"Christ loved the church, and gave himself for it; that he might sanctify and cleanse it with the washing of water by the word."* Eph. 5:25/26. A missionary was once showing us some pictures of natives and he explained that these people were so dirty simply because they had little water. It came as a shock to us to realise how awful it would be if we could not keep ourselves clean because water was so scarce! As our bodies are washed by the use of water, so our hearts and minds can be cleansed through the pure Word of God.

Blessed be the fountain of blood,
To a world of sinners revealed;
Blessed be the dear Son of God:
Only by His stripes we are healed.
Though I've wandered far from His fold,
Bringing to my heart pain and woe,
Wash me in the blood of the Lamb,
And I shall be whiter than snow;

Whiter than the snow!
Whiter than the snow!
Wash me in the blood of the Lamb:
And I shall be whiter than snow!

Father, I have wandered from Thee,
Often has my heart gone astray;
Crimson do my sins seem to me -
Water cannot wash them away.
Jesus, to that fountain of Thine,
Leaning on Thy promise I go!
Cleanse me by Thy washing divine,
And I shall be whiter than snow!

E. R. Latta.

PRAYER

Blessed LORD, I praise Thee for the cleansing power of Thy Word, and Thy love. Amen.

NINETEENTH DAY

Read: Psalm 119:145-152

"I cried unto thee with my whole heart; hear me, O LORD: I will keep thy statutes." v.145.

Yes, here are those words again: *"with my whole heart."* You will find them six times in this Psalm: verses 2, 10, 34, 58, 69 and 145.

Many years ago, searching for more of God and His plan for my life, I was directed in my reading to Jeremiah 29:11-13. These verses illustrate for us what those two words, *'whole heart'*, can mean. *"I know the thoughts I think toward you, saith the LORD, thoughts of peace, and not of evil, to give you an expected end. Then shall ye call upon me and ye shall go and pray unto me, and I will hearken unto you. And ye shall seek me, and ye shall find me when ye search for me with all your heart."* This is an illuminating passage: first note God had a plan already in His mind for His people's good. His plan was a plan of peace, not evil, to give them an expected end. But now note God's method for bringing His plan to pass; they were to seek Him with all their heart. *"Ye shall seek ME, and ye shall search for ME with all your heart."* Seek the Blesser rather than the blessing! As we seek the Blesser, His blessing comes! It is sometimes a good plan to stop seeking for things, and seek GOD. Matt. 6:33, *"Seek ye first the kingdom of God and His righteousness, and all these things shall be added unto you."*

Now read each of those verses in which we have this thought of seeking God, or His Word, with the whole heart. *"Hear me, O LORD, I will keep thy statutes."* This is a prayer of consecration.

Let me come closer to Thee, Lord Jesus,
Oh, closer day by day;
Let me lean harder on Thee, Jesus,
Yes, harder all the way.

Let me show forth Thy beauty, Jesus,
Like sunshine on the hills;
Oh, let my lips pour forth Thy sweetness
In joyous sparkling rills.

Yes, like a fountain, precious Jesus,
Make me and let me be;
Keep me and use me daily, Jesus,
For Thee, for only Thee.

In all my heart and will, O Jesus,
Be altogether king;
Make me a loyal subject, Jesus,
To Thee in everything.

Thirsting, and hungering for Thee, Jesus,
With blessed hunger here,
Longing for home on Zion's mountain,
No thirst, no hunger there.

J. L. Lyne.

PRAYER

O LORD, my God, I come in all sincerity to seek Thee. How I praise Thee that I can come and plead the merits of Christ my Saviour. Praise Thy Holy Name.
Amen.

TWENTIETH DAY

Read: Psalm 119:153-160

"Consider mine affliction, and deliver me: for I do not forget thy law." v.153.

"Plead my cause, and deliver me." v.154.

"Quicken me." "Quicken me." "Quicken me." v.154,156,159.

Although David loved God, and sought to walk in His ways, there were times when he felt his need of a fresh experience of the life of God both spiritually and physically. I think we all feel this as we go on with God. Instinctively in his need the Psalmist goes to God in prayer: *"Consider mine affliction, and deliver me." "Plead my cause, and deliver me."* Here is a man who knows that God is on his side, and He is the God of deliverances! I was greatly helped recently when a friend passed on to me Zephaniah 3:17 Revised Standard Version: *"The LORD, your God is in your midst, a warrior who gives victory."* We sometimes need to grasp afresh this assurance of God's presence, and of His victory over every affliction. Have you been feeling a bit dull and lifeless lately? If so, be reminded of this lovely word in Zeph. 3:17. Then pray, *"Quicken me"*. Note we have this three times in this section. Pray it now: *"Quicken me, quicken me, quicken me."* The word means: to revive, to bring to life. In Ephesians 2:1 we read, *"And you hath he quickened who were dead in trespasses and sins."* This means we are given spiritual life. In Romans 8:11 we again have this word, but this time it is used in the sense of being revived. *"Shall quicken your mortal bodies by His Spirit that dwelleth in you."* Our spirits can be renewed by His Holy Spirit, and our bodies refreshed by that same indwelling Spirit until one day they will be changed and made like unto His glorified body. Remember the promise: *"They that wait upon the LORD shall renew their strength, they shall mount up with wings as eagles, they shall run and not be weary; they shall walk and not faint."*

Under the burdens of guilt and care,
Many a spirit is grieving,
Who in the joy of the Lord might share,
Life everlasting receiving.

  Life! Life! eternal life!
  Jesus alone is the giver:
  Life! Life! abundant life!
  Glory to Jesus for ever!

Burdened one, why will you longer bear
Sorrows from which He releases?
Open your heart, and rejoicing, share
Life more abundant in Jesus.

Oh, for the floods on the thirsty land!
Oh, for a mighty revival!
Oh, for a sanctified, fearless band,
Ready to hail its arrival!

W. Leslie.

PRAYER

The Lord's Prayer.

O Lord, in times when my soul is tempted, and my body is tired, I pray: Quicken me afresh by Thy gracious Spirit. Amen.

TWENTY-FIRST DAY

Read: Psalm 119:161-168

"Seven times a day do I praise thee because of thy righteous judgments. Great peace have they which love thy law: and nothing shall offend them."

v.164 & 165.

'Seven times a day'. Why seven times?

Here we have an expression which conveys the thought of a heart filled with praise to God. The reason for this will be seen by the spiritual significance of numbers in Scripture.* This is a fascinating subject, and can be a most rewarding study. I have only space to refer to what are called the perfect numbers, 3, 7, 10 and 12. Three is the number of divine perfection, and it is often associated with GOD. *"Holy, holy, holy."* Seven denotes perfection in the sense of completion - seven days make a complete week. The seven branched gold lampstand gave light in the Holy place of the Tabernacle. In the book of Revelation we have seven letters to the churches; seven seals, seven trumpets, seven vials. *"How often shall I forgive my brother, unto seven times?"* asked Peter. Jesus said, *"Unto seventy times seven"*. An emphasis upon complete forgiveness - go on forgiving others as God goes on forgiving you. See also Eph.4: 32. Ten is the number of perfection of divine order. Ten commandments, ten clauses in the Lord's prayer. Twelve is the number of perfect government - twelve Patriarchs, twelve Apostles. Is there complete and perfect praise ascending to the LORD (seven times a day, as it were) from your heart every day? Do you praise God for His righteous judgments, for His divine providences? The next verse gives us a key to living the praise life. *"Great peace have they which love thy law: and nothing shall offend them"*. Or, *"nothing shall cause them to stumble"* R.S.V. This is how we can grow into living in perfect praise to God: first, love His Word, second, know His peace, and nothing shall offend - you will have nothing to grumble about.

Fill Thou my life, O Lord my God,
In every part with praise,
That my whole being may proclaim
Thy being and Thy ways.

Not for the lip of praise alone,
Nor e'en the praising heart,
I ask, but for a life made up
Of praise in every part:

Praise in the common things of life,
Its goings out and in;
Praise in each duty and each deed,
However small and mean.

Fill every part of me with praise;
Let all my being speak
Of Thee and of Thy love, O Lord,
Poor though I be and weak.

Horatius Bonar,
(1808-1889).

PRAYER

O LORD fill us, we beseech Thee, with adoring gratitude to Thee for all Thou art. We praise Thee for Thy forgiving grace, and Thy watchful care over us day by day. Amen.

---

*Number in Scripture by Dr. E. W. Bullinger. Published Morgan & Scott.

TWENTY-SECOND DAY

Read: Psalm 119:169-176

"I have gone astray like a lost sheep; seek thy servant; for I do not forget thy commandments."

v.176.

All those lovely verses about the Word of God; all those exhortations to growth in grace, yet now we read in the last verse of this Psalm, *"I have gone astray like a lost sheep."* Does it seem strange that this man should have to admit that? Is this something you cannot understand? I think if I give you the hymn first today, that will help in the explanation.

At even ere the sun was set,
The sick, O Lord, around Thee lay!
Oh, in what divers pains they met!
Oh, with what joy they went away!

O Saviour Christ our woes dispel:
For some are sick and some are sad;
And some have never loved Thee well;
And some have lost the love they had.

And none, O Lord, have perfect rest,
For none are wholly free from sin;
And they who fain would serve Thee best
Are conscious most of wrong within.

Henry Twells,
(1823-1900).

You see, with all David's seeking after God, and his great love of His commandments, he is still very conscious of his own weakness and failures. As Henry Twells writes in this hymn, "And none, O Lord, have perfect rest, For None are wholly free from sin; And they who fain would serve Thee best are conscious most of wrong within." How true this is! The nearer we live to God, the more we realise our own sins and failures. *"All we, like sheep, have gone astray, we have turned every one to his own way; and the LORD hath laid on him the iniquity of us all."* Thank God for the cleansing of the blood of Jesus. Thank God we may have victory over sin through the indwelling power of the Holy Spirit. Thank God that by faith in Christ *'sin shall not have lordship over us'*, and we can know the blessing of *'Holiness by faith in Jesus'*; but we must continually look to Christ in our times of temptation or we will stray like a lost sheep. Paul dared not have confidence in the flesh, and neither can we. *"The arm of flesh will fail you, ye dare not trust your own."* Peter never dreamed he would deny his Lord, but how comforting to know that Jesus had prayed for him (see Luke 22:31-32). And Jesus ever lives to make intercession for us. Our Saviour is always seeking His sheep, always seeking to draw us closer to Himself.

Do you sometimes feel like a straying sheep? Have you thought you are such a weak Christian? Then be encouraged by this thought, that David never lost his sense of need. If you are ever ready to say, *"I have gone astray like a lost sheep; seek thy servant; for I do not forget thy commandments"*, you will know that no matter how weak you may feel at times, the Lord will forgive, and strengthen, and uphold you.

PRAYER

O LORD, I just praise Thee for Thy forgiving love and grace. Keep me close to Thee. Amen.

TWENTY-THIRD DAY

Read: 1 Samuel 3:1-10

"Speak, LORD, for thy servant heareth."
v.9.

Three times the LORD called Samuel by name, and three times Samuel mistook the call for a call from Eli. Then Eli, perceiving that the LORD had called him, gave instructions that should Samuel hear the voice again he was to say, *"Speak, LORD, for thy servant heareth."* Samuel went back to bed, and as he lay there in silence he listened for the voice again. This time, we read, *"The LORD came and stood forth, and called as at other times, Samuel, Samuel."* The previous times we read only that the LORD called Samuel. Matthew Henry suggests it now seems there was some visible appearance of divine glory. Somewhat bewildered, and still a little unsure, Samuel replied, *"Speak, for thy servant heareth."* (Not *'Speak, LORD'* v.10). As you read the rest of this chapter it becomes evident that Samuel had no doubts afterwards that this was the voice of God.

"Samuel lay until the morning" (v.15). He could not sleep thinking about what God had told him. The question may arise in the minds of some, 'Does God really speak to us nowadays as He did to Samuel?' For myself, I must say, 'Most certainly He does.' God can make His mind and will known, but we have to be still before Him or else we will not have *'ears to hear what the Spirit saith'* to our hearts. God may even be speaking to us and we, like Samuel at first, are not aware that it is His voice. Note the value of a heart and mind trained to listen. As we read in Habakkuk 2:1-2, *"I will set me upon my watch tower, and will watch to see what he will say unto me, and what I shall answer when I am reproved. And the LORD answered me, and said, Write the vision, and make it plain....."* There are times when we

need to listen, also to "*watch to see what he will say*". Never overlook the listening side of prayer. It was when Samuel lay quiet that he heard the voice of the LORD. It was a turning point in his life, it can be in yours also.

I long to know Thee better day by day,
I want to draw much closer when I pray;
To listen more intently for Thy voice,
To let the things Thou choosest be my choice.

I long to serve Thee better hour by hour,
Depending more entirely on Thy power;
I want to know more fully all Thy will,
To count upon each promise, and be still.

I long to keep more closely at Thy side,
To worship in Thy presence and abide;
I want to rest more calmly in Thy care,
Assured that Thou wilt keep me safely there.

Ada Habershon.

PRAYER

The Lord's Prayer.

O Lord, grant me the blessing of a quiet mind and silent heart that I may hear when Thou dost speak. Amen.

TWENTY-FOURTH DAY

Read: Lamentations 3:22-36

"The LORD is good unto them that wait for Him, to the soul that seeketh him. It is good that a man should both hope and quietly wait for the salvation of the LORD."

v.25-26.

I want to write today a little more about this all important subject of waiting upon God, which I call the listening side of prayer. The main design of these short daily readings is to help folk amid the rush of life to cultivate the good habit of spending a little time quietly in God's presence every day. As your appreciation of this spiritual exercise grows you will no doubt find, or have already found, that you have a desire to spend more time in prayer and reading the Word. In my little book 'Help me Worship' I give a chapter entitled, 'What About The Matter Of Time'. In it is given some valuable hints as to how it is possible to reclaim time which can be used in this way.

It will not be long before those who truly want to hear the voice of the Lord speaking in their hearts, will realise what the Bible means by waiting upon God. Read again what Jeremiah says in these two verses given above, and note how he uses this word *'wait'*. We have to learn to wait upon God in prayer, and this is one of those things we learn to do by doing it! Remember, you cannot wait in a hurry. You will need to contrive to set apart more time for this, but as we saw yesterday, we must watch to see what the LORD has to say to us. We hear quite a lot these days about transcendental meditation. The verb transcend means to surpass, to rise above. Transcendent means incomparable, ideal; and so we have this adjective, transcendental linked to the word meditation (which means to contemplate or concentrate thought) in order to describe a mental attitude which can lift above that which is merely material. However, we need to be very careful of much that is taught about T.M. because it is linked to non-christian cults and philosophical notions which are unscriptural.

The Church has always had its advocates of spiritual meditation of the kind which is in accordance with the Word of God. We owe a great deal to those who have lived ascetic lives in order to reach a high state of spirituality. It is a great blessing to know the principles of Contemplative Meditation which will help us to *'quietly wait upon God'*. This is why I have given a chapter on the subject in my other little book, 'Praying In Our Prayers'. 'WAIT On The Lord' - see Psalm 27:14. As you wait He will lead you into green pastures.

Nearer, still nearer, close to Thy heart,
Draw me, my Saviour, so precious Thou art;
Fold me, oh, fold me close to Thy breast,
Shelter me safe in that 'Haven of Rest'.

Nearer, still nearer, Lord, to be Thine,
Sin with its follies I gladly resign,
All of its pleasure, pomp, and its pride;
Give me but Jesus, my Lord crucified.

Mrs. C. H. Morris.

PRAYER

"Speak, LORD, in the stillness, while I wait on Thee; hush my heart to listen in expectancy." Amen.

TWENTY-FIFTH DAY

Read: Romans 6:1-14

In these last few days which will complete daily readings for a whole year I feel it may be helpful to include some extracts from my Personal Notebook. For many years I have made notes during some of my sessions of prayer and meditation. These have proved of much spiritual value, and recently I have felt led to share some extracts with others who walk in the ways of the Lord.

Extract 1.

"Knowing this, that our old man is crucified with him, that the body of sin might be destroyed, that we henceforth should not serve sin." Rom. 6:6.

"I like O.C. for today, he says: 'It is a great moment in my life when I do decide that just as Jesus Christ died for the sin of the world, so sin must die out in me - not be curbed or suppressed or counteracted, but crucified'. (From 'My Utmost For His Highest', page 101.)

"Knowing this". Thank God it is an accomplished fact! When Christ died, my old nature died. As Paul says in v.10, *"In that he died, he died unto sin once,....."*. V.11, *"Likewise reckon ye yourselves to be dead indeed unto sin,....."*. In Gal. 2:20 the Apostle declares: *"I am crucified ("I have been"* R.S.V.) *with Christ: nevertheless I live; yet not I, but Christ liveth in me: and the life I now live in the flesh I live by the faith of the Son of God, who loved me, and gave himself for me."* This is what O.C. calls, co-crucifixion with Jesus. This is a statement of fact, and is doctrinally true, but I have to make it experimentally true by this faith reckoning. This must be a continuous experience; it is an accomplished fact, but I have to translate that fact into personal experience. It is not a once for all experience, it is a once and for always experience, by

which I mean, because I came into this blessing 40 years ago it does not mean I am still in the experience today, unless I am continuing to exercise faith in this fact that *"I have been, indeed, I am crucified with Christ"*. Thank God I am living in the enjoyment of it, but there have been times when I have failed to do so because of my lack of faith. Every blessed experience of our salvation comes to us because of the grace of God and through faith in the finished work of Christ. *"Reckon ye also yourselves dead indeed unto sin, but alive unto God through Jesus Christ our Lord."* *"Sin shall not have dominion over you."* While I believe it, I can experience it! This is Scriptural freedom from sin."

Holiness by faith in Jesus,
Not by effort of thine own,
Sin's dominion crushed and broken
By the power of grace alone,
God's own holiness within thee,
His own beauty on thy brow:
This shall be thy pilgrim brightness,
This thy blessed portion <u>now</u>.

Frances Ridley Havergal.

PRAYER

"O Lord, the truth that presses its way through all else this morning is the truth about Sanctification. Forgive me if I have imperceptibly shifted from this great purpose. Amen.

(From Knocking at God's Door, by Oswald Chambers).

TWENTY-SIXTH DAY

Read: 1 John 1:9-10; 2:1-2 & 3:1-10

"My little children, these things I write unto you, that ye sin not. And if any man sin, we have an advocate with the Father, Jesus Christ the righteous."
1:2.

Extract 2

"God's purpose for my life is seen in Luke 1:74-75. *"That he would grant unto us, that we being delivered out of the hand of our enemies might serve him without fear, in holiness and righteousness before him, all the days of our life."* These words come in the prophetic utterance made by Zacharias, the father of John the Baptist, when he was filled with the Holy Spirit. I too am to serve God in holiness and righteousness all the days of my life. This does not make me sinlessly perfect, I am just as frail and apt to err as I ever have been; but God's will for me is that I sin not, and thank God, if I do sin I have an advocate with the Father - One who pleads my cause - Jesus Christ the righteous One. 1 John 2:1/2. The glory and wonder of true Scriptural teaching on Holiness is, not that faith in Jesus makes it impossible for me to sin, but that it makes it possible for me not to sin. *"Whosoever is born of God doth not commit sin;* (Amplified Bible - *'deliberately and knowingly habitually practises sin') for his seed remaineth in him: and he cannot sin, because he is born of God."* Cannot, because he will not. This is what brings me into this blessed experience of freedom from sin - *"It is God who worketh within us both to will and to do of his good pleasure."* Phil. 2:13. He gives the will (desire) and enables me to do (gives strength not to sin). Thus I can know what temptation is, but praise God, I can also know what victory is! Blessed truth! Lord, keep me in the enjoyment and reality of it!"

Precious Saviour, Thou hast saved me;
Thine, and only Thine I am;
Oh, the cleansing blood has reached me!
Glory, glory to the Lamb.

Glory, glory, hallelujah!
Glory. glory to the Lamb!
Oh, the cleansing blood has reached me!
Glory, glory to the Lamb!

Long my yearning heart was striving
To obtain this precious rest;
But, when all my struggles ended,
Simply trusting, I was blessed.

Trusting, trusting every moment;
Feeling now the blood applied;
Lying in the cleansing fountain,
Dwelling in my Saviour's side.

Consecrated to Thy service,
I will live and die for Thee;
I will witness to Thy glory,
Of salvation, full and free.

L. M. Rouse.

PRAYER

Blessed Lord, I praise Thee for full salvation from the guilt and power of sin. I praise Thee that moment by moment I am kept in Thy love. Glory, glory to the Lamb! Amen and Amen!

TWENTY-SEVENTH DAY

Read: Colossians 1:1-14

"That ye might walk worthy of the Lord unto all pleasing, being fruitful in every good work,......strengthened with all might according to his glorious power." v.10/11.

Extract 3.

"A PRAYER - O LORD, my God, help me today to find joy and satisfaction in the ordinary things of life. As I offer to Thee this day's toils, I go forth with the knowledge that Thou, the Eternal God, art with me, and within me. I thank Thee for this quiet time in Thy Presence, and for my meditation on Thyself.

Silence.

"Be still, and know that I am eternal life within you." Yes, LORD, I feel Thy life throughout my soul and body, and I thank Thee for this spiritual renewal. I praise Thee for the ability to read and write; and for the gracious benediction of silence. I bless Thee that I can come before Thee in prayer. LORD, use my words this day, spoken or written, to the praise of Thy glory and the edification and comfort of other souls. As I type these stencils, Lord, and as more copies of this book are produced, may Thy life-imparting power flow through all so that the hearts of men and women shall be drawn nearer to Thee. LORD, build them up on their most holy faith; make those, who will read these books, better and stronger in Christian experience. I thank Thee for the writings of others who in Thy marvellous purposes have been used to bring blessing to my own heart, grant that what I now write may be to others what I myself have so often found in books I have read - nothing short of spiritual nourishment by which my own Christian life has been enlarged. How I thank Thee that Thou dost take up the weak things to confound the

mighty, and the things that are not, to bring to naught the things that are; that no flesh should glory in Thy presence. (1 Cor. 26:31.) "Work on then, LORD, till on my soul eternal light shall break; and in Thy likeness, perfected, I satisfied shall wake."

My heart is resting, O my God,
I will give thanks and sing:
My heart is at the secret source
Of every precious thing.

Oh, peace of God that passeth thought,
I daily, hourly sing,
My heart is at the secret source
Of every precious thing.

Now the frail vessel Thou hast made,
No hand but Thine shall fill;
The waters of the earth have failed,
And I am thirsty still.

I thirst for springs of heavenly life,
And here all day they rise;
I seek the treasure of Thy love,
And close at hand it lies.

A. L. Waring.

PRAYER

The Lord's Prayer.

Te Deum Laudamus.

(See Volume 1, page 148.)

TWENTY-EIGHTH DAY

Read: 2 Corinthians 1:8-20

"All the promises of God in him are yea, and in him, Amen, unto the glory of God by us." v.20.
"God that cannot lie." Titus 1:2.

Extract 4.

"Christ is the confirmation of all God's promises to the believer. God gives His promised word, Christ says, Yes, that's true; and we say the Amen (so be it). Or do we always? It saves us a lot of worry when we do believe His Word. I have just been reading O.C. 'My Utmost For His Highest', page 111. Writing about the servant to whom only one talent had been given, (Matt. 25:24-27) he says: *"The servant justified himself in everything he did and condemned his lord on every point"* - 'Your demand is out of all proportion to what you give'. Have we been slandering God by daring to worry when He has said: *"Seek ye first the kingdom of God, and His righteousness; and all these things shall be added unto you."?* Worrying means exactly what this servant implied - 'I know you will leave me in the lurch'.

That, in effect, is what I say to God every time I worry about trifles. This is only a little incident, but worth recording: the Lord gave me victory over fret when I was tempted to worry about a certain matter, quite foolish really, but it is so easy to get a worrying habit! I thought about it, and then said quite deliberately, 'I will not worry about it'. After about half an hour circumstances proved there was absolutely no reason why I should have worried! How glad I was that I rested in the Lord about it. I have been listening to a tape-recorded message by W. F. P. Burton, one-time missionary in the Congo (now Zaire) on this verse - 2 Cor. 1:20. This is good:

Once a £1 note was found with a piece of paper attached on which had been written these words:- This piece of paper in your hand declares to you, that on demand you twenty shillings shall receive (now five-penny pieces). This simple promise you believe, it sets your mind as much at rest as though the silver you possessed. So Christ, who died but now doth live, doth unto you the promise give that all who on His Name believe should everlasting life receive. Upon the first you calmly rest; which is the surest and the best? "Man's Bank may break, God's never can! 'Tis better trust in God than man!"

Souls of men why will ye scatter,
Like a crowd of frightened sheep?
Foolish hearts, why will ye wander
From a love so true and deep?

There is plentiful redemption
In the blood that has been shed;
There is joy for all the members
In the sorrows of the Head.

If our love were but more simple,
We would take Him at His word,
And our lives would be all sunshine
In the sweetness of our Lord.

F. W. Faber.

PRAYER

Lord, I will not worry about that thing - (stop slandering God!) but I trust Thee. Amen.

TWENTY-NINTH DAY

Read: Isaiah 12

"Therefore with joy shall ye draw water out of the wells of salvation."

v.3.

Extract 5.

"If you want to be discontented look within. If you want to be distracted look around. If you want to be delivered look up. Look up to Jesus, He will deliver me from all discontentment about myself, and all distractions of this world. Jesus is also my deliverer from discouragement. With JOY I will draw water out of the wells of salvation today. I was greatly encouraged by the following incident: a visitor to the Chapel this morning spoke to me after the meeting saying she had a message to give me from a Christian lady to whom she had given a copy of my Comfort Booklet, 'Have You Been Wondering Why?'. This person had suffered much pain for a long while, and before she died she asked her friend to tell me what a blessing she had received through reading my booklet. She was helped by knowing it was written by someone who knew suffering, and it seems this lady was particularly helped by my story about going through a tunnel.

How good the Lord is to let me hear about this, especially as I had sent a copy of that one to someone recently and heard that although he had read it more than once he did not get any help from it. Very sad! Oh, how grateful I am that the Lord saved me while I was young; it is going on for 60 years now since I received Jesus into my heart as my own Saviour.

I have just remembered Dr. S. C. Carpenter's paraphrase of Philippians 1:6. It must be twenty-five years ago I first saw this, but whenever I read it my heart is stirred by its simple yet profound truth. Here it is: "The end is not yet, but I am utterly confident that you will persevere. What tells me this? My faith in God! God began it, and God does not leave off doing what he has begun to do; therefore He will finish it! It was a good day's work when God first set your feet in the road of discipleship. He is not going to let you down!" - Lovely, praise God. *"He will keep the feet of His saints."* Jesus saves and Jesus keeps, Hallelujah!"

I've something in my heart that Jesus gave to me,
It makes me feel like singing glory all the day:
He found my captive soul and gave me liberty,
And now I feel like singing glory!

He makes the path grow brighter
Every passing day;
He makes the burden lighter,
All along the way;
His Word is my delight,
His will I now obey,
And all the time I'm singing glory.

O weary heart and sad, O heavy-laden soul,
If you would feel like singing glory all the day,
Just let the Saviour in and let Him take control,
Then you will feel like singing glory.

L. R. Minor.

PRAY AND PRAISE!

THIRTIETH DAY

Read: John 15:5-12

"Be filled with the Spirit."

Eph. 5:18.

"God gives the Holy Spirit to those who obey Him."

see Acts 5:32.

Extract 6.

"This experience of the filling (or fullness) of the Holy Spirit comes, by the grace of God, to me through faith and obedience. *"We are his witnesses of these things, and so also is the Holy Spirit whom God hath given to them that obey him."* I find a passage from one of the writings of the late Dr. F. B. Meyer most helpful so I will copy it in here. "God does not fill with His Holy Spirit those who believe in the fullness of the Spirit, or those who desire Him, but those who obey Him. Man would rather work for God than walk with God; its not so costly. It is easier to employ the hands than to discipline the heart!" How true that is! I found this in a magazine the other day, it is entitled, For Greater Usefulness. "A bar of pig iron costs one dollar. If this bar is hammered into horseshoes through the furnace and on the anvil, it's value becomes three dollars. If the same bar of iron is further processed through the fire, water, and hammer, and refined into steel, it can be made into a sword worth three hundred dollars. If the same bar of iron were further refined and drawn into watch springs it then becomes worth many thousands of dollars." What amazes me is that it can be the same bar of iron, but the difference is in its having yielded to the design in the mind of the master craftsman, and its being put through the fire, and under the hammer, and in the case of the watch-springs its being rolled and stretched, and drawn out in order to make it fit for the purpose for which it was intended.

What a lesson! The secret of obedience is that

we shall abide in Christ, and to abide in Him simply means yielding to Him. Costly to the flesh, but it is not working for God that is of greatest value to Him but it is walking with God. Then as we walk with Him He can use us for whatever purpose is in His Mind, and we shall be 'workers together with Him'.

Walking with Jesus day by day,
Taking Him for our Guide;
Holding His hand we can never stray
Far from His wounded side.

Looking to Jesus day by day,
Ever for fresh supply,
Never a blessing will He delay,
Naught but in love deny.

Speaking for Jesus day by day,
Telling what He has done;
Helping some wanderer to find the way,
Guiding some erring one.

Singing for Jesus day by day,
Praising His Name in song;
Telling His love in a happy way
Gladly the whole day long.

Mary Ann Shorey.

PRAYER

Lord Jesus, teach me that the path of usefulness is the path of greatest obedience. Amen.

THIRTY-FIRST DAY

Read: Romans 12:1-16

"Rejoice in your hope, be patient in tribulation, be constant in prayer."

v.12 R.S.V.

Extract 7.

"Lord, I worship and adore Thee."

Silence

Prayer: O God, set our hearts at liberty from the service of ourselves; and let it be our meat and drink this day to do Thy will; through Jesus Christ our Lord.

I change the collective pronoun in this prayer to the singular personal pronoun: 'set my heart at liberty'; 'let it be my meat and drink this day to do Thy will, Amen.'

Evil men give themselves, body soul and spirit, over to Satan. It is terrible to contemplate, but we have in this country now those who worship Satan! At one time we would have only associated that with heathen idolatory in other lands. A spiritualistic medium gives up himself, or herself, to be controlled by a familiar spirit. That is an utter abomination to God (Deut. 18:10-12).

Good men give themselves, spirit soul and body, to God. In Romans 12:1-2 we see that this is for Christians, *'our reasonable service'*, or *'our spiritual worship'*. A consecrated Christian gives himself over to be controlled by the Holy Spirit of God. The difference is, while a spiritualist medium loses all self-control, a consecrated Christian gives himself to God and is controlled by the Spirit without losing his self-control. God never sets aside human personality, He is willing always to work through our human personality. Therefore a person acting under the influence of the Holy Spirit will never say or do anything which will bring discredit upon the truth of the Gospel. Others may not always understand him, the unconverted did not understand what was going on when the early disciples experienced the out-pouring of the Holy Spirit, Acts 2, but those who accused the disciples of being drunk were wrong. Peter could easily explain from Scripture what was happening, and the result was that thousands were converted to Christ and they too received the Holy Spirit (v.38/39). When we were young there was a favourite hymn in the Sankey hymnbook (618) and it comes to my mind now, so I will write two verses."

Yielded to God, my body, soul and spirit,
Oh, what rejoicing fills my peaceful breast;
All, all is well, no doubt or fear disturbs me,
While on His promise now alone I rest.

Yielded to God, my life and its devotion,
Yielded the service of each day and year;
Oh, what a peace pervades my every feeling!
Oh, what sweet visions on my sight appear!

Fanny J. Crosby.

PRAYER

"God be in my head, and in my understanding;
God be in my eyes, and in my looking;
God be in my mouth, and in my speaking;
God be in my heart and in my thinking;
God be at my end, and at my departing.
Amen."

NO. 1 EXTRA

Read: John 21:15-25

"Simon, do you love me?" "Yes, Lord, you know that I am your friend." ..... "Feed my lambs". "Simon, do you love me?" "Yes, Lord, you know that I am your friend." ..... "Feed my sheep". "Simon, are you my friend?" Peter was deeply hurt because Jesus' third question to him was, *'Are you my friend?'*, and he said, *'Lord, you know everything, you know that I am your friend'."*

(J. B. Phillips v.15,16,17.)

Shall we look at these verses closely? Three times Jesus asked Peter if he loved Him, three times he is made to confess his Lord. Some see here a threefold confession in the place of Peter's sad threefold denial. That may well be, but I think there was a little more in the Master's questioning than that. Our word 'love' is terribly over-worked, it is made to stand for all sorts, and degrees, of loving, whereas in the original language of the New Testament there are two words which can mean love but they are not interchangeable. We lose this in the A.V. and also in the R.S.V. I see. J. N. Darby and J. B. Phillips, and others bring out this subtle difference. This is interesting, and helpful. There is a play on words here. First Jesus said to Peter, *"Do you love me?"* - meaning love with an intense, personal devotion. Peter evidently could not trust himself to confess that kind of deep love, after what he had done by denying the Lord. So he uses the weaker word, which means love in the sense of friendship, friendliness. *"Yea, Lord Thou knowest that I am attached to you."* (Darby). J. B. Phillips puts it: *"You know that I am your friend."* Twice Simon Peter said that - it was all he felt able to say! You will have wondered why Peter was grieved when Jesus asked him a third time, *"Do you love me?"* The reason was that that time Jesus used the word that Peter had been using. "Then the third time Jesus said,

'Simon, son of John, are you my friend?' Peter was deeply hurt because Jesus' third question to him was, *'Are you my friend?'*, and he said, *'Lord, you know everything, you know that I am your friend'*." Then the third commission, "*Feed my sheep*".

I feel sure many will agree with me that the life of Peter afterwards proved he really did love Jesus with a love that was deep, strong personal devotion. He could not bring himself to say it, but he did it! You may feel like that: "*Lord, it is my chief complaint that my love is weak and faint, yet I love Thee, and adore, Oh, for grace to love Thee more.*"

So let us finish these thoughts on John's Gospel using this hymn as a prayer:

My Jesus I love Thee, I know Thou art mine,
For Thee all the pleasures of sin I resign;
My gracious Redeemer, my Saviour art Thou,
If ever I loved Thee, Lord Jesus, 'tis now.

W. R. Featherston.

PRAYER

Spend a little while silently loving the Lord, and feeling His love for you.

NO. 2 EXTRA

Read: John 20:26-31

"Thomas answered and said, My Lord and my God."
v.28.

It was a lovely holiday that year. The weather was perfect, the Guest House was in an ideal setting high up at Lynton, North Devon. I stayed with Principal Percy G. Parker whose spiritual help and guidance just then was a real blessing to my soul. It was good for me, as a young minister, to be able to have fellowship with one whose spiritual experience was so much greater than mine. I came back to London refreshed, not only physically, but spiritually also.

On the Bookstall a little card printed in red attracted my attention. I purchased one and stuck it in the front of my Bible. I have it still although the date registers it was forty years ago! It is a reminder of a spiritual land-mark in my life. I thought if I gave a reproduction of that card it could be a help to you now, as it was to me those many years ago, and I might say still is a help. So here it is:-

A VICTORIOUS LIFE

"This is the VICTORY that overcometh the world, even our FAITH."
1 John 5:4.

"Reckon ye also yourselves to be dead indeed unto sin, but alive unto God, through JESUS CHRIST OUR LORD."
Romans 6:11.

"I am crucified with Christ, nevertheless I live: yet NOT I, but CHRIST LIVETH IN ME: and the life which I now live in the flesh, I live by the FAITH OF THE SON OF GOD, who loved me, AND GAVE HIMSELF FOR ME."
Gal. 2:20.

V I C T O R Y

"Moment by moment, I'm kept in His love,
Moment by moment, I've life from above,
Looking to JESUS till glory doth shine,
Moment by moment, O LORD, I am Thine."

"I take Thee blessed LORD,
I give myself to THEE:
And Thou, according to Thy Word,
Dost undertake for me."

Signed: ....

Date: ....

"THOMAS SAITH UNTO HIM, MY LORD AND MY GOD!"

Will you say that to the Lord Jesus, NOW?

This book has been produced by the EMMANUEL TRUST in conjunction with our publishers Moorley's Bible & Bookshop Ltd., Derbyshire, whose work on this series is much appreciated. For particulars of the EMMANUEL TRUST please write to the author c/o the publishers.

OTHER BOOKS BY THE SAME AUTHOR

PRAYING IN OUR PRAYERS
HELP ME WORSHIP
PEACE & CALM IN THEE WE FIND
WHEN WAVES SWAMP THE BOAT
HERE IS GLORY IN PLACE OF GLOOM
FROM A PASTOR'S NOTEBOOK NO. 1 & NO. 2.

COMFORT SERIES

I WONDER WHY?
IN LOVING SYMPATHY
BEAUTY OF SPRINGTIME
BEAUTY OF AUTUMN LEAVES
THE GREATEST FRIEND
HOW TO COPE WITH FRUSTRATION.